IF THIS WERE A DREAM, WHAT WOULD IT MEAN?

Discovering the Spiritual Meaning
Behind Everyday Events

IF THIS WERE A DREAM, WHAT WOULD IT MEAN?

Discovering the Spiritual Meaning
Behind Everyday Events

By

Murray Dueck

FRESH WIND PRESS

Edited by Kevin Miller (www.kevinwrites.com)
Cover design and layout by Andrew B. Jaster (www.ajaster.com)
Front cover photo and author photo by Noel Alsop.

Printed in Canada by Friesens (www.friesens.com)

Third Printing

Library and Archives Canada Cataloguing in Publication

Dueck, Murray, 1965-
If this were a dream, what would it mean? : discovering the spiritual meaning behind everyday events / Murray Dueck.

Includes bibliographical references.
ISBN 0-9733586-7-X

1. Revelation. 2. Bible--Evidences, authority, etc. I. Title.

BT103.D83 2005   231.7'4
C2005-903305-3

Fresh Wind Press
2170 Maywood Court
Abbotsford, BC, Canada
V2S 4Z1

www.freshwindpress.com

Table of Contents

SECTION III: READING THE GREAT AUTHOR'S MODERN WORKS

THE POWER
OF SYMBOLS

Symbolism has always intrigued me. The way God weaves symbols and foreshadowing together through prophetic words, dreams, visions, pictures, and even human history is astounding. God authors history the same way he authors other forms of revelation, using symbolic language and powerful metaphors to shape our understanding of him.

Throughout Scripture, we read many examples of how God speaks in symbolic language, as Numbers 12:6 says: "Then he said, 'Listen to my words: When a prophet of the LORD is among you, I reveal myself to him in visions, I speak to him in dreams'." God spoke to Pharaoh in a dream that only Joseph could interpret. The same thing happened with Nebuchadnezzar and Daniel. Joseph of Nazareth also had a dream about his betrothed, Mary, during which an angel said, in essence, "Marry the girl!" That dream changed Joseph's mind, because prior to the dream, he was doubtful about her pregnancy (cf. Matthew 1). The so-called "three wise men" were warned in a dream to avoid King Herod. Later on, Joseph had another dream instructing him to take Mary and Jesus to Egypt, also to avoid Herod. These were very practical, very prophetic dreams that contained real spiritual power and an impetus for change.

But God is too wise to focus simply on dreams as a means of communication with us. His hand can be seen working throughout history, even in seemingly random events. God has his own unique "sign language" that every Christian ought to learn and reflect upon.

Murray Dueck's work with Samuel's Mantle—his prophetic school—as well as the principles he has written in this book; have greatly enhanced my understanding of God's symbolic language. Over the past few years, I have spent a lot of time with Murray in his home church in Langley, BC, and he has visited me in California. He is a man who loves the prophetic revelation that God has given him. He is hungry to receive from God, and the Lord has honored that desire with more and more insight into how he works. Murray is a man swimming with reckless abandon in the deep things of God.

Murray has dedicated his life to training people in the prophetic. His school has grown from a single class with students from a couple of churches to a regional presence with classes every day. He is hungry for fresh, prophetic manna, and he has helped inspire that same hunger in the lives of his students.

One of the intriguing principles in this book is Murray's focus on how God's hand works in current events. The stories and news accounts he has included provoke us to pray for our cities, states, countries, and governments. God is at work in everything. If we have eyes to see him moving, we can partner more effectively with what he is doing.

Even a casual reading of Scripture reveals that God invented the literary device of foreshadowing. Murray shows us that our mission as prophetic Christians is to recapture and relearn that language of symbols, metaphors, and signs. Knowing what God wants to do will provoke us to pray, fast, and work toward seeing his kingdom established on earth. These symbols, as Murray will teach you throughout this wonderful book, can be learned only through spending time with God. As we give him our dreams, visions, and prophetic impressions, God develops our ability to see him working in places we never would have dreamed.

One resource for such symbols and metaphor is our dreams. Dream interpretation is a gift produced by meditating on our dreams and then asking God for his take on them. "Daniel had understanding in all visions and dreams," says Daniel 1:17. One of my closest friends has a gift of interpreting dreams. If you are a dreamer, write down your dreams and work through them with God. Open them up for comment and prayer. Your dreams may not seem relevant in the moment, and a few weeks down the road, you may want to put them on the shelf. But you ought to get in the habit of writing things down; treating your dreams as you would any other type of revelation, because you never know when they will be called upon.

Visions, which are closely related to dreams, are another source of revelation. Sometimes, revelation comes through such pictures or even through moving scenes. Many of us have probably had such experiences. Some visions speak to us through everyday objects and may even use our own understanding of these things to speak prophetically. In Jeremiah 1:11–12, we witness this kind of vision:

> *"The word of the LORD came to me: 'What do you see, Jeremiah?'*
> *'I see the branch of an almond tree,' I replied. The LORD said*
> *to me, 'You have seen correctly, for I am watching to see that my*
> *word is fulfilled'."*

When God asked the prophet what he saw, Jeremiah looked around and noticed the almond tree branch. It was a perfectly common sight, totally unremarkable. However, the interpretation, timing, and specific need of the people combined to produce a positive and significant prophetic interpretation.

I had a similar experience once, also involving a tree. I was about to speak to a meeting of several hundred people when the Lord directed me to a young woman in the middle aisle. I asked her to stand up. As she did, God showed me a picture of a hazel tree. I knew the type of tree it was, because my father and I had been landscape gardeners. All I had was this picture, so I asked the Lord, "What do you want to say?" There was nothing, so I started in with what I knew: "I'm seeing a picture of a hazel tree," I said, and then I began to describe its properties from memory. "It has beautiful flowers and fruit. It can grow almost anywhere. It's resistant to disease, and its bark and flowers can be used for medicinal purposes, as a tonic or a sedative that brings comfort from pain. It's very hardy and resilient."

As soon as I came to the end of that statement, I knew what God wanted to do. "That's how God sees you," I continued, "He thinks you're beautiful and that you're going to bear good fruit in your life. You mustn't worry that you're no good. You're tough and able to resist the enemy. You'll grow in almost any situation." As I moved prophetically, she cried, and her friends cheered and laughed.

I finished prophesying, prayed for her, and taught my seminar. At the end of the meeting, she came to me. "Thanks for what you said. You don't know this, but my name is Hazel," she told me. Apparently, that same afternoon, she and her friends had been drinking tea, and Hazel had been in a bad mood. "Hazel. Stupid name, Hazel," she had said. "Why couldn't I have been called by a prettier name? I hate it, and I wish I could change it."

God, in his incredible sense of humor, had used me to say, "Excuse me, but I chose your name. I gave it to you, and I gave it to you for this purpose." She told me that she had cried, because she realized that her name had been given to her for a reason. When she was in the womb, God had named her Hazel. What a powerful word from a perfectly ordinary and common source.

Metaphors and signs that flow from dreams, visions, history, and current events play a key role in the supernatural development of people and the communities to which they are joined. In Scripture, this practice of invading the logical world with supernatural communication is widespread and commonplace, almost ordinary. What is *not* ordinary (yet) for the Church is an awareness and acceptance of this form of revelatory communication and the ability to interpret it. This is why I believe Murray's book—including his life and ministry—is going to be a significant key to unlock all that the Father would reveal in these fascinating and difficult times.

The world has hijacked the realm of symbolism to such an extent that it is now almost despised in western Christian thinking. But in the Bible, God speaks through symbols and metaphors that need interpretation. Jesus, himself, used parables repeatedly to share the deep things of the kingdom. He has always spoken in this way and will continue to do so. "He who has ears to hear; let him (or her) hear!" If the Church will not listen to revelatory language, the Lord will speak to the world directly, as he did with Pharaoh and Nebuchadnezzar. How many people in our society and culture are starting to have amazing experiences in a revelatory spiritual context? They need the correct interpretation. And such an interpretation can only come from practitioners in this heavenly, pictorial language, people like Joseph and Daniel. Through their understanding of God's symbolic language, these two ordinary people turned the fortunes of God's people at critical times through their alignment with God in understanding dream language. The New Age movement has taken revelatory language prisoner, but God is in the business of setting captives free. The Father has given some of those keys to Murray. He is sensitive to the Spirit and has a passion for freedom and release.

Enjoy this book, and then, if you get the opportunity, connect with the author himself. You will find him delightful, enthusiastic, humble, wise, and loads of fun. He will make you think, laugh, and aspire to be quiet before the Lord so that he may commune with you. Murray is a great teacher. He is unafraid to tackle issues that prevent the development of prophetic assets to the Church and community at large. Murray's work, experience, and meditation on the elements of symbolism, foreshadowing, metaphor, and parable will greatly increase your understanding of every method of revelation. I hope this book will help shape you and many other prophets, leading you into a deeper faith in God. It is our destiny to see the world through eyes that understand God's symbolic language and actions. It is our job to ask continually, "If this were a dream, what would it mean?"

Graham Cooke
Vacaville, CA
April 2005

PARADIGMS AND PARADIGM-SHIFTS

FORESHADOWING

The Jordanian prince's horse was out of control. It spun and kicked, refusing to be subdued. The harder Crown Prince Hassan's staff tried to control it, the more frenzied the horse became. It kicked and bucked, raising a cloud of stinging dust until it finally broke free from its master's men and plunged into the Red Sea.

This was a strange thing for a horse to do, especially since it was now swimming toward a war zone that no living creature had been able to cross and survive. It was even stranger, seeing as the horse had a saddle on its back and iron shoes on its feet. Why would it choose to go for a swim instead of dashing out into the wide-open desert behind it?

Nevertheless, the horse swam away from its Arab master for two kilometers until it reached the Israeli city of Eliat on the opposite shore of the bay. An Israeli police boat guided the weary animal over the last few meters of its journey. Once on shore, the horse allowed itself to be led away peacefully by its new friends, a people who, minutes earlier, had been the horse's enemy.

A great beginning to a novel don't you think? Suspense, imagery, action, tension, and a true story at that! But was this also a portent of things to come? A foreshadowing? Perhaps.

Foreshadowing: A Tool in the Hand of the Master

Foreshadowing is a literary device that uses symbolism to hint at things to come. Authors use this technique all the time to create suspense and anticipation in readers, hooking their interest by providing them with clues that will help them unlock the mystery to come.

Have you ever seen the movie *Independence Day?* At the beginning of the film, the shadow of a huge alien ship covers the moon and the Apollo landing site. The ground shakes, erasing the Apollo moon rover's tracks from the dust. In that moment, the signs of man's presence on the moon are obliterated. The camera points back to the ship as it moves toward earth. Will the signs of man's presence on earth be erased as well?

How about in *The Empire Strikes Back,* when Luke Skywalker enters the cave on Dagobah during his training with Yoda? Yoda warns him not to go inside, but Luke goes anyway. Suddenly, Luke hears the hiss of a light saber igniting. Then, out of the shadows steps Luke's archenemy—Darth Vader! Luke ignites his own light saber, and they duel. Luke gains the upper hand and lops off Darth Vader's head. When Vader's head tumbles to the ground, his mask breaks open, revealing Luke's face! What does this portend for the future? Perhaps Luke should have listened to Yoda after all!

Here is one more example: In the movie *You've Got Mail,* everything was going wrong for Meg Ryan's character, who owned a small, independent bookstore. Things were so bad she finally had to close the store. Before she locked the door and walked away for the last time, she recalled a happier time when she danced with her mother in the store. Then she walked down the road, lost and alone in the dark. Fade to black.

When the next scene faded in, we saw a cherry tree in full bloom. The sun was shining; it was the beginning of a new day. What could this mean? Could this be the beginning of a new season for Meg as well? Spring is a time when things come back to life. Spring is also the season of love.

Enter Tom Hanks' character. Up until now, he had been Meg's nemesis. Just as the sun caused the cherry tree to bloom, would love now bloom between these former enemies? Only time would tell.

Two Ways of Looking at the Situation

Now that you have a better sense of what foreshadowing is, let's apply it to the story of Prince Hassan's horse. Taken on one level, this incident could be viewed as just another strange event, something you might hear about on *Ripley's Believe It Or Not*. Indeed, that is exactly how many people viewed the event—as an anomaly. But they could not deny the symbolic nature of the event. As a spokesman for Israeli Prime Minister Yitzhak Shamir noted at the time, "Horses know no boundaries.... We see no reason why we should not follow in the footsteps of the Jordanian horse who sought friendship with Israeli horses."[1]

The story I have just described took place in April 1992. The media took note of it because of the unique relationship between Jordan and Israel at the time. In truth, Jordan and Israel didn't really have a relationship. They were still in a state of declared war. Since Jordan and Israel didn't recognize each other's existence, Israel couldn't even give the horse back themselves. They had to get a UN soldier to do that. This is what made the item so newsworthy. In fact, when the horse first swam over the border into Israel, the Israeli army officers checked the horse for bombs, thinking it was a trick!

Taken on another level, this story could also be seen as a form of foreshadowing, a literary device used by the Great Author to foreshadow what was about to happen between Israel and Jordan. That is exactly how I see this story, as a precursor to God's hand stretching across the Jordan River—a hand of peace, not war. You may not believe me right now, but you may feel differently once you hear the outcome of this story, which is rather unbelievable. Like the beginning of any novel, this symbolic event merely pointed toward what was to come.

What most people didn't realize was that behind the scenes, secret peace negotiations between Jordan and Israel (facilitated by an American mediator) were just beginning. Consider the odds of such an event ever happening: Libya, Syria, Iraq, Iran, Lebanon, Saudi Arabia, and virtually every other Muslim nation surrounding the Holy Land had sworn to push Israel into the sea, to blot out their very existence. It was unthinkable at the time that Jordan would betray its Arab brothers and declare Israel a friend.[2] But within two years, the war between the two countries would be over. Jordan and Israel would become friends, making Jordan only the second Arab nation (after Egypt) to recognize Israel's right to exist.

Who could ever think of such a thing? God, the Great Author, the Writer of history. He had thought of such a thing, and two years before Israel and Jordan signed the historic peace treaty, he gave the entire world a peek at what was to come by having Prince Hassan's horse do the miraculous: swim through a war zone that no human being would have dared to cross. Not only did the horse get through to the other side, he emerged from the water and stood with the Jews in peace! This horse, trained to serve only its Arab masters, even let a hated Jew lead him around—and he appeared to like it! The horse wouldn't let its Arab masters handle it that way. What an embarrassment, and on national television for every Arab and Jew in the world to see! But that was the point: The Great Author wanted everyone to know he was about to write a new chapter in his book on the Middle East. And, as authors do, he used the tool of foreshadowing to catch his readers' attention, to pique their curiosity, and to make them hungry for the story to come.

The particular symbol God used in this case was a prince's horse, a symbol of power that was given over to the enemy in peace. This should not be surprising. In the Bible, horses often symbolize strength (cf. Psalm 20:7; Isaiah 31:1; and Jeremiah 12:5). Things haven't changed much. We still measure a machine's power in terms of horses—horsepower!

The prince's horse running away from its master and into the hands of the enemy depicted what was about to transpire between these two nations: the end of war and the beginning of peace. If you were charged with writing a novel about Israel and Jordan, could you come up with a better example of foreshadowing? But this was more than a mere literary device. This event had eternal significance. God designed this symbolic event for his people to see and interpret. He wanted the readers of the Divine Author's work to know he was going to change the structure of Middle Eastern politics. And he wanted us to respond accordingly—through prayer.

Not An Isolated Incident

Does God use the instrument of foreshadowing often? Yes! In this book, we will look at many examples of how God uses symbolic language to foreshadow what he is about to do so that we can partner with him through prayer. He does this on personal, local, national, and international levels—and he has been doing it since the beginning of his dealings with us. But before we can begin to recognize such foreshadowing, we must learn how to look deeper into events in our lives and in the world at large. We must learn to understand God's symbolic language so we are able to see beneath the surface of events and interpret what we find there. We must undergo a "paradigm shift," developing the ability to view the world from God's perspective. Only then will we be able to read the Great Author's works.

At this point, you may still be thinking the incident with the prince's horse was nothing but a highly symbolic coincidence. Even so, I urge you to hear me out. Having read and experienced many of the Great Author's works in my own life and in the lives of others, I am certain that once you read and experience them for yourself, you will begin to think otherwise. In fact, my hope and prayer is that by the end of this book, the word "coincidence" will be erased from your vocabulary, because you will have begun to live with "eyes wide open," able to see and experience the Great Author's presence in every area of life.

Don't Give Up!

God is so big and beyond our understanding that sometimes I think we simply give up. We stop trying to make sense of things and get on with our daily lives. We wonder if God still speaks and how we fit into his plan. But we have given up trying to answer those questions.

I am here to tell you that God does still speak and that he does still have a plan for your life, your church, your community, your nation, and the world. He really is on your side! In a sense, that is what this book is about: to make God BIG in your eyes again, to bring you back to the point where you really believe God is in control, that he really is above the nations, that nothing flusters him or leaves him unmoved. All that, and he wants his people to hear him, to work with him, and to watch his mighty acts among the nations. God wants you to feel like you are intimately involved in this work—because you are!

[1] "Israel returns Jordan's royal steed," *The Province,* April 10, 1992, p. A31.

[2] Regional politics prevented King Hussein from revealing his more moderate policies toward Israel. In particular, Jordan was dependent on Iraq for oil, had a large Palestinian Arab population hostile to Israel, and was faced by constant pressure from Syria, who wanted nothing to do with Israel.

Chapter One

THE POWER OF
PARADIGMS

I t is the glory of God to conceal a matter; to search out a matter is the glory of kings. (Proverbs 25:2)

Take a look at the following drawings. What is the first thing you see in each one of them? Now look again. Do you see something different?

Here's a tip: In the first picture you should see a man playing a saxophone. In the second picture, you should see a man with glasses looking at you, and in the third picture, you should see a face of a young lady turned away from you.

This is not all there is to these pictures. Each picture also contains a secondary, hidden picture. I have placed these pictures in order from easiest to hardest.

Look again. In the first picture, you should also see a lady's face. The black splotch floating by itself on the right of the picture is her left eye, and the bottom of the saxophone curls around her chin, which is white. Do you see her now?

In the second picture, many people see a man's face at first. However, the picture also spells the word "liar." The glasses are the "L," the "I" forms the nose, the "A" is the man's mouth, and the "R" is his neck.

The third picture is more difficult. At first, most people see it as a picture of a young lady. But look closer, and you will also see an old woman. The young lady's necklace forms the old woman's mouth, the neckline of her dress outlines the old woman's chin, and the young lady's ear is actually the old woman's eye. Can you see her now? If you still can't see the old woman, try blotting out the young lady's eyelash.

Now, for all of you keeners, here is a difficult one:

I'm sure all of you see an old man with ivy for hair and a long beard. But can you also see the young couple kissing in a garden? I'll let you keep looking for a while before I give the answer.

These pictures are a fun way to illustrate how many things in life can be interpreted in more than one way. The same image or event can have two completely different meanings—one on the surface and another hidden, deeper meaning that is usually more difficult to find. Trying to see the second image in each one of these drawings is a good way to begin training your mind to look beyond the surface of events to discover what the Great Author is up to. As you read this book, take the lessons you have learned from these pictures and apply them to the examples given. Look deeper. What is God saying? What has he hidden within events that are occurring right under your nose? You will discover a brand new world you never realized existed.

The Image of the Lovers in The Old Man

Speaking of noses, let me help you with the image of the old man. I saved this image for last, because I think it makes a strong symbolic statement of what I am trying to convey in this book.

Many of us see life much like we see this old man: dull, tired, and gray. However, hidden within this picture is an image of romance, love, and intimacy—two lovers, a bride and a groom. To me, this is a powerful illustration of how learning to read God's symbolic language also allows us to see the love and excitement that lurks just beneath the dull, gray surface of life. If we are able to undergo such a paradigm shift, we will also be able to see our loving, Heavenly Bridegroom in everything that happens around us.

Can't see the lovers yet? Try this:

- First, block out the old mans hair so you can't see it anymore.
- Look at the old man's nose. It is the center of activity for the young, kissing couple. The left nostril makes the woman's shoulder while the bridge of the nose makes her face.
- The young man's face is made from the area just beneath the left eye.
- The old man's eyes make the hair for both young people.

- The old man's upper lip is the young man's arm. The maiden's arm is the left part of the old man's mustache.
- The maiden's dress is the old man's beard. The young man's cloak is the old man's mustache on the left side of his face. Can you see them now?

We are involved in a divine love affair with the Groom, Jesus Christ. And we, the Church, are his Bride. If we begin to see the Lord in everything around us, we will be swept up into that love affair. Life will no longer be the "same old, same old." Once again, it will become a divine romance between Christ and his Bride. We will see what our Groom is doing on the earth and go forth hand-in-hand, as we become partners in his dealings with humankind. Does this sound like a paradigm you would like to have? If so, then read on, and be prepared to gain a new way of looking at life!

On the Look-out for a New Paradigm

When you first looked at the pictures with the hidden images you had a certain point of view, or in other words a certain paradigm. As you looked harder at the pictures, your paradigm began to shift. In fact, with the picture of the old man you went from an old worn-out looking paradigm to a new, vibrant, and romantic paradigm. Everything in life is like that. We see things at first from our own point of view, or paradigm, but as time goes on, we can see what others see from their point of view as well. When we can finally grasp someone else's point of view, we have experienced a paradigm shift. To begin to see events from God's paradigm, to see the deeper meaning in events around us, we must first gain an understanding of what paradigms are, how paradigms affect us, and where paradigms come from. Once we understand how our paradigms function, we will be ready to see God's paradigm, the hidden picture God puts right in front of us everyday. We will be able to shift from our paradigm to God's, and life will be transformed from the "same old, same old" into a divine romance.

The Problem of Paradigms

Everyone views the world through his or her own, unique paradigm. A paradigm, also known as a "worldview," is a system of beliefs, assumptions, concepts, values, and practices that help us organize our world. Generally, your paradigm or worldview is shaped by religion, culture, education, family, peers, and significant events in your past. Paradigms include beliefs and assumptions about all sorts of things. For example, if you live in North America, chances are your paradigm includes beliefs like "all people are created equal," "capitalism is good, communism is bad," and "marriage is a union between one man and one woman" (although this last notion is being challenged presently).

For the most part, paradigms are a good thing. By organizing life in this fashion, paradigms allow us to absorb new information and experiences without becoming overwhelmed. As we go through life, we don't have to evaluate and define every new thing we encounter. We merely hold it up against the grid of our paradigm and file it in the appropriate category. For example: Everyone's paradigm contains a category called "dog." Even though dogs come in all shapes and sizes, whether we encounter a poodle or a Great Dane, we do not have to stop and figure out what this new creature is each time we encounter a dog. We simply recognize the basic components of which all dogs are comprised and file the information accordingly. Paradigms also show us how to respond to a given situation. When we encounter a dog, for instance, we know that bending down and holding out our hand for them to sniff is a good way to introduce ourselves. We also know that no matter how big or how small the dog is, we will probably become friends with it rather quickly by offering it a treat or scratching it behind the ears.

Despite their positive function, however, our paradigms can also work against us at times. As our experience with the drawings above demonstrates, sometimes we can get so mired in one way of looking at things that we have a difficult time seeing life from a different perspective. We forget that our paradigm isn't the only one, and that it may not even be the best one. While our paradigms allow us to see certain things well, they also blind us to other things.

No one surrenders his or her paradigm without a fight. How could we? Our paradigm is our primary source of security and comfort. It is our map of the world. Whenever a new experience, new information or a new person comes along and challenges our paradigm, we find it extremely stressful. Generally, we deal with such situations by reclassifying the experience so it fits into our paradigm, discrediting the disruptive information or simply avoiding the situation altogether. But such responses are only effective for so long. Sooner or later we must adjust our paradigm to incorporate the new experience. Whenever that happens, we undergo what is called a "paradigm shift."

Shifts Happen

In his highly influential book *The Structure of Scientific Revolutions,* philosopher and historian Thomas S. Kuhn (1922–1996) coined the term "paradigm shift" to describe the nature by which scientific progress is made. Contrary to popular belief, Kuhn argued that the history of scientific progress is not composed on an incremental increase in knowledge but as a series of revolutions whereby one long-standing paradigm, or belief system of how the world works, is replaced by a new paradigm that is incompatible with the first.[1] Put in layman's terms, a paradigm shift helps us to step outside of our current worldview and into another one. Our location doesn't change, just the framework or lens through which we experience it. When you first observed the drawings in this chapter, you saw them a certain way. But as your eyes adjusted and you began to see the second image, you developed a new view. You had a paradigm shift. You were looking at exactly the same black lines on white paper, but you began to see them in a completely different way. This same process happens all the time as we journey through life.

A Simple Example

The easiest and best example of a paradigm shift is one you may have already experienced: your conversion. Do you remember what that was like for you? Suddenly, or perhaps over a period of time, the world went from a place controlled by chance and luck to a highly ordered and structured creation. The world you lived in didn't change, but how you perceived it certainly did. On how many levels did that paradigm shift affect your view of life? Think how it altered your views on relationships, your career, your hobbies, and your goals in life. Suddenly, you saw the "picture within the picture," something that had been in front of you all along but which you had failed to notice—the fact that a loving God was intimately involved in every detail of your life. Not only that, I bet you could look back on your life and see the hidden work of the Divine Author as he wrote your personal story long before you became a Christian. Before your conversion, your life may have seemed like a jumble of incoherent events. But after meeting Jesus, you could see how the Lord had protected and guided you long before you even acknowledged his existence. All at once, you saw the story the Great Author had been writing about your life. You had a paradigm shift—you gained a brand new worldview—and it was positively delightful!

Having kids is another great example of a paradigm shift. Any parent can attest to that. When you become a parent, everything changes—traveling, sleeping, eating, how you spend your free time (What free time?), and so on. You also gain a new appreciation for what your parents went through for you. You appreciate the children's workers at church, you develop an entirely new set of interests, and you develop a new reason for living. A paradigm shift!

A funny thing about paradigm shifts is, once you begin seeing things in a new way, there is no going back! Of course, you can still see things the old way, but there is no way you can "un-see" the secondary image. Once you accomplish a paradigm shift, you always have it. You have developed the habit of looking deeper. That is the goal of this book, to help you develop a deeper perception of the world. It will change the way you see the world around you. Most importantly, it will enable you to see God as the all-powerful, ever-present being that he is.

How Do Paradigm Shifts Happen?

For the most part, paradigm shifts are beyond our control. Our paradigms begin to shift without our knowledge and without us willing them to do so. Some of the examples I cited above illustrate this well. For instance, while having children is a conscious choice (usually), the various ways children affect your life is not. Starting out, you have no idea how these crying, squirming, cooing bundles of humanity are going to worm their way into your heart. It just happens. Suddenly you find yourself crying at movies that feature touching parent-child relationships, you can talk endlessly about diapers and toilet training, and you begin to restructure your entire life in order to maximize sleep. Other examples of incidents that cause involuntary paradigm shifts include getting married, the death of a loved one or entering another culture. To use an extreme example, imagine what would happen if a flying saucer actually did touch down on the White House lawn. Talk about an involuntary paradigm shift! Suddenly, it becomes painfully clear that we are not alone in the universe. Time to revise your worldview!

But paradigm shifts can also take place on a conscious level. Yes, even though we tend to cling to our paradigms at all costs, in some cases we can actually will ourselves to see the world in a new way. That is exactly what happened with the drawings I showed you earlier. You knew there was more to the images than met the eye, and you consciously chose to search until you found the second picture. This point is central to what I am going to teach you in this book. Life is not much different than those drawings. On the surface, you see one thing. But if you look deeper, you will discover something completely different, and often more significant. While the idea may still seem radical to you—you're still clinging to your old paradigm, after all—beneath the events you observe and experience in your life, in your community, your nation, and in the world lies a secret, symbolic language known only to God and to the people who know how to read it. Are you one of those people? You can be. And this book will show you how.

---

[1] Thomas Kuhn, *The Structure of Scientific Revolutions, 2nd Edition.* (Chicago: University of Chicago Press, 1970), p. 175. This paradigm shift does not just involve the rejection

of the dominant theory. Kuhn argues that it may actually change the world in which scientists conduct their work by casting that world in an entirely new light. For example, when Copernicus (AD 1473–1543) proposed a Sun-centered solar system rather than an Earth-centered one, he did not just add to our knowledge about the movements of the planets against the apparently fixed background of stars. His theory demanded that we completely revolutionize our understanding of how the universe is structured and how we fit into it. His theory was not just additive, it was transformational—not to mention controversial.

Chapter Two

SYMBOLISM, GOD'S LANGUAGE OF CHOICE

In 1991, The United States accomplished an amazing feat: It won the Gulf War against Iraq with almost zero combat fatalities. In fact, more soldiers died as a result of accidents in Iraq than in battle. The world was stunned. Saddam Hussein had promised the "mother of all battles." Instead, he was dealt the "mother of all losses."

President Bush had staked his election on a victory in Iraq, and he won it convincingly. The United States was able to shake off the clinging shame of the Vietnam War by beating Iraq and demonstrating what a superpower they really were. Following the victory, President Bush was so high in the opinion polls he was considered unbeatable. No American president had ever won a major war and then lost his position when it came time for re-election. Thus, it was unthinkable that George Bush, a president who had not only led the world into war but also lost only a handful of men in the process would ever get voted out of the White House. But that is exactly what happened. In 1993, the Great Author turned the page on the United States to start writing his next chapter. Things were going to change, and the foreshadowing of what that change would look like was plainly visible long beforehand to those who could read the Great Author's writing.

If This Were A Dream, What Would It Mean?

A Fateful Visit to Japan

With the war over, now it was time to focus on other things. The top priority? The US economy. In 1992, President Bush traveled to Asia to drum up business. While he was in Japan trying to get the Japanese to open up their markets to US goods, divine foreshadowing struck...

Picture the scene: President Bush had just spent a wonderful day playing tennis with the Japanese Emperor and other dignitaries. Now it was time for a formal banquet to begin. The President was sitting next to Japanese Prime Minister Miyazawa Kiichiof when the President became violently ill. His head rolled to the side, his face became ghastly white, and then he vomited and passed out. Luckily, he suffered no permanent injury. The President could have fallen to the floor. Instead, Prime Minister Kiichiof grabbed the President on the way down and propped him up on his lap. It seemed like every newscast and newspaper in the world carried the image of the sick president with his head cradled by the wide-eyed Japanese Prime Minister. This event was seen as a national embarrassment for the US. But was that all there was to it? Why did this tale of weirdness captivate the world's attention and imagination?

Seeing the Big Picture

The American economy was ill, and President Bush had gone to Japan for help. Instead, he became ill and had to be propped up by the Japanese Prime Minister! The Japanese certainly didn't miss the symbolism of the moment. Consider this excerpt from the *New York Times*:

> *The vivid and dramatic image of Mr. Bush struggling in the arms of the Japanese Prime Minister seemed likely to make an indelible impression on the Japanese people, especially since it came after a trip in which the United States has been asking for steps to help its weakened economy.*
>
> *The symbolism of the seemingly strong Mr. Bush collapsing was even compared by some to the widespread impression in Japan*

that the United States is reeling under the recession and is asking Japan to take steps to help it recover.

"It's so symbolic," said Naohiro Amaya, a former deputy Minister of the Ministry of International Trade and Industry, appearing on television tonight. "The superpower America is tired and everyone around has to take care of it."[1]

Sure enough, over the next few years the Japanese poured millions of yen into the US economy to keep it afloat during the recession. By 1993, Japan was holding two-thirds of America's foreign debt.[2] The way the Japanese "propped up" America's ailing economy was remarkably similar to how the Japanese Prime Minister had propped up George Bush in Japan.

Eventually, things reached the point where Japan refused to lend any more money to the US. Then things got really ugly. Following the Gulf War, US companies were shedding employees like a snake sheds its skin. Times were tough, and the blame for the sick economy was placed at the feet of none other than President George Bush. To save the American economy and boost his chances of re-election, Bush had turned to Japan to hold him up. They tried, but it was no use. Despite his unparalleled popularity following the war, Clinton defeated him soundly on the grounds of the sick economy. What better foreshadowing of the future than the US President passing out and being held up by the Japanese Prime Minister? A movie or novel could do no better.

Just Tell Me!

If God had something to say through this event, why didn't he just tell us straight out? This is an important point. Have you ever wished Jesus would just appear in your bedroom or your church and reveal all of life's mysteries? What's it all about? Why am I here? Where am I going? How can I solve the dilemma I am currently facing? Guess what: Even if Jesus did take you out for coffee and tell you all of these things and more, you likely wouldn't understand a word of it. He could look you straight in the eye and tell you exactly what you wanted to hear, but you just wouldn't get it.

Don't believe me? Have you ever decided to do something differently than you have in the past, only to hear your spouse or a close friend exclaim, "I've been trying to tell you that for years!"? Maybe you decided to spend less time at work, to stand up to your overbearing parents or simply to get more exercise. People may have been trying to tell you to do it for a long time, but your current paradigm prevented you from hearing them. Something else had to happen—a paradigm shift—before you could finally see your situation the way they saw it. As every twelve-step program teaches, the first step to dealing with your problem is admitting that you have one; and the first step to admitting you have a problem is a paradigm shift.

Another reason why I believe you wouldn't understand Jesus if he told you things straight out is because few people in the Bible understood Jesus when he spoke plainly. Their paradigms kept getting in the way. Oddly enough, the people who best exemplify this spiritual dullness are the same men who spent the most time in direct contact with Jesus—his disciples.

When the disciples were arguing about who was going to be the greatest in heaven, Jesus brought forth a small child and told them that unless they became like little children, they would not make it to heaven (Mark 10:13-16). Another time, he told them that to be great in heaven, they had to become the servant of all (Mark 9:35). But even though Jesus gave them these clear, direct answers to their questions, the disciples went right on arguing and asking the same questions. They didn't get it. Jesus also told the disciples over and over that he was going to suffer and die, but they didn't understand that either. Their paradigm told them that the Messiah would lead them in a rebellion against their Roman oppressors. There was no room in their worldview for a suffering Savior, one that would overcome his enemies by dying, not by killing.

In Acts 1, the disciples were still wondering when Israel would reign over her enemies. Even after everything Jesus told them about himself came true, the disciples remained trapped in an earthly worldview. Jesus did not come to establish an earthly kingdom; he came to establish the

Kingdom of God, which was not of this world. These men, hand-picked by Jesus to be his closest friends and confidantes for three years, still didn't know what he was talking about much of the time. The reason? A conflict of paradigms. Jesus' goals were heavenly; theirs were still earth-bound.

What does this mean for us? As I said earlier, many of us are stuck in the belief that if Jesus were with us physically—if he went on Larry King and answered all of our phone calls—somehow we would understand everything completely. But this runs counter to the biblical report. Having Jesus in their midst did not help the disciples understand Jesus one bit better than we can understand him now. Proximity to Jesus was neither the solution nor the problem. What made the difference was the paradigm through which the disciples viewed Jesus. Once they were able to overcome their earth-bound paradigm and grasp God's heavenly perspective, they were able to decode what Jesus was saying. All it took was for them to stop seeking their own advantage and start seeking the source of all good things, which is God. This is great news for us. Even though we can't sit down with Jesus face-to-face (at least not in a physical sense), we have the opportunity to hear and understand him just as clearly as the disciples did! All it takes is for us to overcome our own faulty paradigm.

Learning to see the picture within the picture as we did with the drawings in chapter one is fun. But real paradigm change can be scary, because it demands that we give up our comfort and security and step forward into the unknown. Even those of us who are most inclined toward risk and adventure have a tough time when confronted with such ambiguity. Realizing this, God is more than willing to help us move beyond our faulty paradigm so we can begin seeing things from his divine perspective. His method of choice? Symbolic language.

I think many people believe God uses symbolism to confuse us, to punish us, and even to keep us from understanding him. But in fact, God uses symbolic language for exactly the opposite reason: to help us understand. It is the only way to help us get past the false paradigms that keep us separated from him. Symbols force us to move beyond the rational part of our brain, upon which we have become so accustomed to relying, and search out what is truly going on. But God doesn't want us to find just information. Through our search, he wants us to find him.

The question of why God uses symbolic language makes sense only from from a Western paradigm. As Westerners—even as Christians—we have adopted a scientific approach to life. For us to believe something, it must be testable and predictable. If it can't be seen, felt, tasted, touched or heard, for all practical purposes, it does not exist. While this aspect of our paradigm serves us well in some areas, it hurts us in others. Even when presented with logical proof about something, if the proof doesn't fit the grid of our current paradigm, we tend to shrug it off. Another central problem with the Western, scientific paradigm is our tendency to divide the world into two categories: sacred and secular. We think church is sacred; work is secular. Prayer is sacred, entertainment secular. Marriage is sacred, science secular. What few people recognize is that *this is not a biblical concept.* To the writers of the Bible, everything was sacred. Nothing happened apart from God. Everything was through him and to him. In addition, the biblical writers did not distinguish between prophetic interpretation of dreams, visions or actual events. To the Jewish mind, God enveloped all realms, not just the invisible. "From him and through him and to him are all things" (Romans 11:36). Therefore, physical events—such as what happened to President Bush—could have just as much prophetic meaning as a dream or vision.

Signs = Symbolic Language

In fact, the Jews had a word to describe the sort of thing that happened to President Bush. Our word "sign" would be its modern equivalent. They used this word whenever they sensed God was speaking to them symbolically through the events around them.

> *Jesus did many other miraculous signs in the presence of his disciples, which are not recorded in this book. But these are written that you may believe that Jesus is the Christ, the Son of the*

living God, and that by believing you may have life in his name.
(John 20:30–31)

Signs in Scripture can be broken down into three categories:

1) Signs that cause people to see the natural realm as representing the spiritual realm: Special days, ritual acts, and memorials. Signs in this category include the Passover, baptism, and communion.
2) Signs that confirm the Word of the Lord and prove his trustworthiness. The rainbow is a good example of this sort of sign.
3) Signs that proclaim what the Lord is about to do on earth, fingerprints that reveal God's involvement in human affairs. The virgin birth, the star that appeared when Christ was born, and the outpouring of the Holy Spirit on the day of Pentecost all fall into this category.

Think of signs as a form of "heavenly language," symbolic events that need to be interpreted so we can see the spiritual meaning behind them. The purpose of this language, as we shall see, is to demolish our old, false paradigm and replace it with a paradigm based on God.

Signs Are Given to Help You See What You Can't See Otherwise

A good example of how God used signs to help people get past their false paradigms is the series of strange events surrounding Jesus' death on the cross. Up to this point, the Roman soldiers charged with guarding the crucifixion victims viewed Jesus as just another Jewish troublemaker getting what he deserved. It seemed like someone or other was always claiming to be the Messiah, promising deliverance from the Romans. But this time, things were different. When Jesus gave up his spirit, subsequent events led even these hardened Roman soldiers to realize their assessment of Jesus could not be further from the truth:

And when Jesus had cried out again in a loud voice, he gave up his spirit. At that moment the curtain of the temple was torn in two from top to bottom. The earth shook and the rocks split. The tombs broke open and the bodies of holy people who had died were raised to life. They came out of the tombs, and after Jesus' resurrection they went into the holy city and appeared to many people. When the centurion and those with him who were guarding Jesus saw the earthquake and all that had happened, they were terrified and exclaimed, "surely he was the son of God!" (Matthew 27:50–54)

The events described above are what the Jews called "signs": symbolic events that were full of heavenly language. Most Christians today have no trouble interpreting these signs, such as the temple veil ripping in two. The veil separated the Holy of Holies, where God dwelt, from everyone else. Only the High Priest could enter this partitioned area, and even then only once a year. The moment Jesus uttered the words, "It is finished"(John 19:30), the veil was torn from top to bottom, signifying that humankind was no longer separated from God. Jesus' death gave us direct access to God once again, just like Adam and Eve had enjoyed in the beginning (cf. Hebrews 6:19; 10:24).

The other signs are equally easy to interpret:

- Tombs breaking open: This proved that Jesus had power over the grave.
- The righteous coming back to life: This proved that a righteous life in God was rewarded with new life, indeed, eternal life.
- After three days, the resurrected went to Jerusalem: Jerusalem was the Holy City, where the king reigned, where the Messiah would reign. On the day Jesus was resurrected, these people appeared in Jerusalem to bear witness to the power of Jesus. This was a sign to Jerusalem that Jesus was alive, that he had power over death, and that he gave eternal life.

Seeing and interpreting these signs and realizing they were connected to Jesus' death on the cross caused the Roman soldiers to have a paradigm shift. Jesus wasn't a Jewish troublemaker after all; he was the Son of God. The signs proved it. The signs—heavenly language—given by God in connection with Jesus' death clearly stated that Jesus had power over death, that the righteous in Christ would live again, and that access to God had been granted.

Just as God used symbolic language to help give deeper meaning to Jesus' death on the cross, he continues to do the same thing today. In fact, God has been using signs or symbolic language to speak to his people from the beginning.

Plagued by the Plagues

One of the clearest biblical examples of God using signs to break an old paradigm is the story of the ten plagues (Exodus 4—9). You have probably heard this story ever since Sunday school. That's part of the problem. Stories like this have become so familiar that we don't really listen to them anymore. Like the drawings we looked at in chapter one, we have a difficult time believing there really could be a picture within the picture. But I invite you to look at this story again, this time on a symbolic level.

> For by now I could have stretched out my hand and struck you and your people with a plague that would have wiped you off the earth. But I have raised you up for this very purpose, that I might show you my power and that my name might be proclaimed in all the earth." (Exodus 9:15–16)

God wanted the Egyptians to have a paradigm shift, to step into a new worldview, to move from pride to humility. But first, their old, false paradigm would have to go. God would bring about this paradigm shift by speaking to the Egyptians through signs.

The Ten Plagues

Each plague was another sign in a prophetic timeline that would culminate in the Egyptians realizing there was only one true God in Egypt—the God of Abraham, Isaac, and Jacob.

> *But I will harden Pharaoh's heart, and though I multiply my miraculous signs and wonders in Egypt, he will not listen to you. Then I will lay my hand on Egypt and with mighty acts of judgment I will bring out my divisions, my people the Israelites. And the Egyptians will know that I am the Lord when I stretch out my hand against Egypt and bring the Israelites out of it."* (Exodus 7:5)

Here is a list of the plagues in the order they occurred:

- Plague 1: The Nile turns to blood (Exodus 7:17)
- Plague 2: Frogs (Exodus 8:1–15)
- Plague 3: Lice (Exodus 8:16–19)
- Plague 4: Flies (Exodus 8:20–32)
- Plague 5: Death of livestock (Exodus 9:1–7)
- Plague 6: Boils on man and animal (Exodus 9:8–12)
- Plague 7: Thunder and hail: (Exodus 9:13–35)
- Plague 8: Locusts (Exodus 10:1–20)
- Plague 9: Darkness (Exodus 10:21–29)
- Plague 10: Death of Egyptian firstborn (Exodus 11:1–9)

My first question after seeing this list is; why would plagues be a sign to the Egyptians? Why not use some other means to get the Egyptians' attention? Second, why these particular plagues? Third, why this particular order? Were they chosen at random, or did God have some sort of logical progression in mind? Before we can venture an answer, we must first gain a better appreciation for the ancient Egyptian paradigm. How would they have interpreted these signs? If signs are heavenly language, then what did these plagues mean to the Egyptians?

The Egyptian Worldview

To the Egyptian mind, a pantheon of gods controlled the world. Much like Hindus today, the Egyptians had a god for everything: life, death, crops, water, fertility, animals… You get the idea. Herodotus (484–425 BC) called the Egyptians "religious to excess, far beyond any other race of men."[3] They believed everything that happened was the result of some deity or another. Between these gods and man was Pharaoh, whom the Egyptians believed was the incarnation of the gods. He was backed up in turn by the priests and their magic. The Egyptians believed that worshipping these gods was what made them a superpower. This knowledge is the key to unlocking the symbolism of the plagues.

With each plague, God wiped out one or more of the main Egyptian gods. When the plagues were complete, the Egyptians finally saw that their gods, their Pharaoh, and their priests were completely powerless, and that Yahweh was God over all! Put another way the Egyptians had a paradigm shift brought on by God using signs! "For at this time I will send all my plagues to your very heart, and on your servants and on your people, that you may know that there is none like me" (Exodus 9:14).

To make this point a little clearer, I will list the plagues again, this time explaining their significance from the Egyptian point of view.

- *Plague 1: The Nile turns to blood.* The Egyptians saw the Nile River as the god who supplied the lifeblood of Egypt. Gods associated with the Nile included Hapi, Hatmehyt, and Osiris, among others.[4] The power of these gods was broken as Yahweh took control of the river, making the Nile a source of death instead of life.
- *Plague 2: Frogs.* Frogs were associated with the fertility goddess Heqt, who had the body of a woman and the head of a frog. During the second plague, frogs became a curse for the Egyptians instead of deities to be worshipped. Just as it is unlawful for Hindus to kill cows or remove them from stores, so it was with the Egyptians in regard to the frogs. The frogs went into every corner of every house, but because of their religious

beliefs—their false paradigm—the Egyptians were powerless to stop them.

- *Plague 3: Lice.* One of the chief Egyptian gods was Geb, god of the earth. Offerings were given to Geb to ensure the bounty of the soil. As you will recall, the lice were produced when Aaron struck the ground with his staff, thus producing lice from the dust (Exodus 8:16–17). Geb should have been able to defend his domain, but once again, God rendered yet another Egyptian god completely powerless.

  One of the effects of the lice would have been that the Egyptian priests would be unable to serve their gods in their temples.[5] The Egyptian priests would now be ceremonially unclean, and their gods would be proven powerless to intervene. At this point, the priests finally buckled, saying, "This is the finger of God" (Exodus 8:19).

- *Plague 4: Flies.* Scholars believe that the word often translated as "flies" in this passages actually means all kinds of different biting and stinging insects.[6] Insects were also worshipped as gods in Egypt. Utachit was the god of flies, and Khepra was often shown as a scarab beetle. The Egyptians thought that worshipping the gods who controlled these insects would keep the insects from attacking them. But it didn't work out that way this time. In fact, this was the first time Pharaoh himself asked Moses to pray to Yahweh on his behalf (Exodus 8:28).

- *Plague 5: Death of livestock.* The Egyptians worshipped livestock just as Hindus today worship cattle and other animals. In fact, the Persians won a significant battle against the Egyptians by driving sacred animals in front of them. The Egyptians would not fight for fear of harming the sacred animals, so the Persians were able to wipe them out. By killing the animals in this fashion, God demonstrated that he was greater than these domesticated gods. Two of the Egyptian gods decimated by this plague were Hathor, the cow-headed god that protected cattle herds, and Apis, the bull god.[7]

- *Plague 6: Boils.* With this plague, God instructed Moses to scatter ashes toward the heavens (Exodus 9:8–10). This was God's declaration of war on the sky gods of Egypt: Horis, Shu, Isis, and Nut. It was also a custom of the Egyptian priests to scatter ashes from sacrifices as a sign of blessing. Moses was mimicking the priests, but his actions brought boils, not blessings. Exodus 9: 11 specifically points out that the Egyptian priests were infected with boils and could not stand before Moses and Aaron. In other words, God made the Egyptian priests a public laughing stock. The people used to go to them for help, but now they were inflicted just like any common Egyptian or slave. Their cleansing rituals did nothing for them. In fact, they couldn't even get off the ground! On top of that they were once again banned from their own temples because of their physical uncleanness.

- *Plague 7: Thunder and hail.* Think of Egypt as a desert country that was fortunate enough to have a river running through it. Thus, rain, hail, and thunder were virtually unknown in the region. It must have come as quite a shock then to see fiery hail fall from the sky. Where were Nut, Horus, Shu, and Isis, the sky gods of Egypt, who were supposed to protect against such things? Exodus 9:31 tells us that the flax and barley crops in Egypt were wiped out. An Egyptian celebration was held at this time of year called the "coming out of Min." Min was the god who protected agriculture. But his party probably had to be cancelled that year. At this point, even Pharaoh began to recognize the distinction between the gods of Egypt and the God of the Hebrews.

> *"I have sinned this time. Yahweh is righteous, and my people and I are wicked. Entreat the Lord, that there may be no more mighty thundering and hail, for it is enough" (Exodus 9: 27b–28a).*

- *Plague 8: Locusts.* Locusts were pretty much a standard "judgment against sin" in the Old Testament. However, the Egyptians had found a way around locust infestations. They had a god named

Serapia whose job was to keep them away. If the Egyptians worshipped this god, all would be fine. In addition to Serapia looking after the locusts, the god Nepri also looked after the grain. Anubis was guarding the fields, and Ermulet looked after the crops. It looked like the Egyptians had their bases covered. But God proved them wrong. Exodus 10:4–6 says the locusts covered the face of the earth and even filled all of the Egyptians' houses. They destroyed everything, just as Yahweh had destroyed the gods who were supposed to keep the locusts at bay.

- *Plague 9: Darkness.* "Then the Lord said to Moses, 'Stretch out your hand toward heaven, that there may be darkness over the land of Egypt, darkness which may even be felt'" (Exodus 10: 21). One of Egypt's chief deities was the sun god Ra or Amon-Ra. The Egyptians believed that at night, Ra went through the underworld fighting his way through darkness and storm to re-emerge the next day. If Ra didn't return, that meant creation was over.[8] By restricting the sun from shining for three days, God showed the Egyptians that Ra had nothing on him. I should also point out that Pharaoh was considered to be Ra's son, meaning that when the darkness fell, Moses could brag to Pharaoh, "My dad is bigger than your dad!"

- *Plague 10: Death of firstborn.* This was the straw that broke the Egyptians' back. The ancient Egyptians used to pray for the protection of their firstborn children. They believed the gods protected these children supernaturally, because they would inherit the family wealth and name. Pharaoh even married his own sister to keep the bloodline pure. They believed the son produced by this union would also be part of "god's family" and divinely protected. Through this plague, Yahweh showed once and for all that he alone—not the Egyptians' false gods—had the power of life and death. It was on this day that the festival of the Passover was instituted.

As you can see, by the time all ten plagues were through, the Egyptians got the message loud and clear: Their gods were "toast." The Egyptians gave the Hebrews whatever they asked for, just as long as they agreed to leave (Exodus 12:36).

Remember: The purpose of God's symbolic language is to help us see what we cannot see otherwise, to help us undergo a paradigm shift. At first, God had Moses and Aaron make their request to Pharaoh's face (Exodus 5). They spoke to him plainly. But Pharaoh could not hear a word Moses and Aaron said. That's because Pharaoh saw Moses and the Israelites through the faulty paradigm of his culture, tradition, religion, and history. Who were these slaves and their god to tell him what to do? The only way God could get through to this guy was to dismantle his worldview piece by piece. Pharaoh was a tough sell, but as the signs began to multiply, even he bent his knee eventually. God works the same way today. He keeps multiplying the signs until we can see our false paradigm, understand why it is wrong, and let go.

The View from the Street

How would a poor Egyptian peasant, living hundreds of miles from the capitol, perceive these events? I am certain that even if such a person never heard the details of what transpired between Moses, Aaron, Pharaoh, and the priests, he or she would have been able to read the signs and understand. Something significant was happening to the nation, and nothing less than a comprehensive overhaul of the nation's belief system would be required to comprehend it fully. This period would have been extremely unsettling. As each god was dethroned, the peasant would turn to another god—only to see that one dethroned as well!

The perspective of the Egyptian villager is important for us to consider, because in terms of most significant world events, we are in a similar position today. We don't know all that goes on behind the locked doors of power, but we can see and interpret the signs God continues to provide in our day and age. God wants us to know what is going on behind the scenes. Stories like this one from the Bible teach us how God dealt with people in the past so we know what to expect in the present. Knowing this, we can pray into these events according to his will, possibly even affecting their outcome.

Where Do False Paradigms Come From?

To answer this question, we need to go right back to the story of Adam and Eve. Humans did not always have a distorted worldview. There was a time when we had it right. In the Garden, walking with God in the cool of the day…

> *Now the Lord God had formed out of the ground all the beasts of the field and all the birds of the air. He brought them to man to see what he would name them; and whatever the man called each living creature, that was it's name. So the man gave names to all the livestock, the birds of the air, and all the beasts of the field. (Genesis 2:19–20)*

As you can see, back then humankind had a great relationship with God. God even let Adam name all of his creatures. Think of all the animals, birds, fish, and insects there are on earth. How long would that have taken? It didn't matter, because God and Adam enjoyed working together, walking together, and talking together. They saw each other as friends, and that is exactly how they spoke to each other: face-to-face.

Genesis 2:21–25 records the creation of Eve. Now Adam had a perfect mate. It is interesting to note that at first, Adam had no problem with viewing God or each other through the eyes of innocence and purity. "The man and his wife were both naked, and they felt no shame" (Genesis 2:25). Their paradigm was clear and faultless, just like a perfect pane of glass. God was good, he was on their side, and Adam and Eve loved each other. Sounds like Paradise, doesn't it? Unfortunately, everything was about to change.

Genesis 3:1–6 recounts how Satan, disguised as a serpent, deceived Adam and Eve in the Garden. It is at this point when the first false paradigm of God was introduced to humankind. Satan convinced Eve that God couldn't be trusted, that he was withholding information in order to control them, that they could be just like God if they ate the forbidden fruit. Unfortunately, the moment Adam and Eve acted on this advice, that clear pane of glass started to crack and fog up. First, it ruptured their relationship with God. Then it damaged their relationship with each other: "Then the eyes of both of them were opened and they realized they were naked; so they sewed fig leaves together and made coverings for themselves (Genesis 3:7). And, finally, it disrupted their relationship with Creation as a whole (Genesis 3:17–19).

Adam and Eve had a paradigm shift. The world hadn't changed, and neither had God. But suddenly, they were seeing everything in a new way—a bad way. They had always been naked and thought nothing of it. But now they were ashamed. Afraid. Their inability to see clearly caused Adam and Eve to make decisions and take actions that would have been preposterous a short while ago. And then God showed up… "Then the man and his wife heard the sound of the Lord God as he was walking in the cool of the day, and they hid from God among the trees of the garden" (Genesis 3:8).

For the first time, Adam and Eve saw God not as a friend but a threat, someone to fear. That clear pane of glass grew even darker.

> *"But the Lord God called to the man, "Where are you?"*
> *He answered, "I heard you in the garden, and I was afraid*
> *because I was naked; so I hid." (Genesis 3:9–10)*

Here we get a closer look at what was going on in Adam's mind. Adam heard God, and for the first time, he was afraid. He made a decision that was fear-based, a decision that only hours earlier would have been unthinkable, but which now seemed completely logical based on this new paradigm of fear and shame. What did Adam do? He hid.

> *And He said, "Who told you that you were naked? Have you*
> *eaten from the tree that I commanded you not to eat from?"*
> *Then the man said, "The woman you put here with me—she*
> *gave me some fruit from the tree, and I ate it."*

Then the Lord God said to the woman, "What is this you have done?"
The woman said, "the serpent deceived me, and I ate."
(Genesis 3:11–13)

In this last section, we find another result of Adam and Eve's paradigm shift: blame-shifting. Adam blamed Eve, and Eve blamed the snake. From Adam and Eve's new point of view, this sort of behavior made sense. After all, they had just moved from a God-centered paradigm to a self-centered one, so now everything was about looking out for number one. That was the lie Satan sold them. Everything that happened to Adam and Eve, from the bite of the forbidden fruit onwards was based on a paradigm of self-fulfillment, self-protection, and self-preservation. "I eat, I hide, I cover my shame with fig leaves, I blame-shift."

Before Adam and Eve's paradigm shift—commonly referred to as "the Fall"—they enjoyed a close relationship with God, and they could talk openly together. After the Fall, God could still speak directly to Adam and Eve as he had done before, but they could no longer hear him. All they could see and hear was their own fear and shame. God had lost a friend, and Man had gained an enemy—or so he thought. The pane of glass went completely black.

The First Use of Symbolic language

The situation was far from hopeless though. In fact, right in the midst of pronouncing a curse on Adam, Eve, and Satan, God offered a glimmer of hope. Man had changed how he related to God. Now God was going to change how he related to Man. If God could no longer speak to his creatures directly, he would introduce a new way of speaking, a form of communication that would enable his message to slip past our faulty paradigm and into our hearts and spirits. There was but one stipulation: The only people who would be able to understand this new language would be those who sought after the truth. Those who just wanted information would not get the message. A person had to be seeking the source of that information: God. This new language was called "symbolism," the language of dreams and visions, signs and wonders. "It is the glory of God to conceal a matter; to search it out is the glory of kings" (Proverbs 25:2).

This new symbolic language first appears when God utters his response to Adam and Eve's unfaithfulness:

> *So the Lord God said to the serpent, "Because you have done this,*
>
> *"Cursed are you above all the livestock and all the wild animals! You will crawl on your belly and you will eat dust all your life.*
>
> *And I will put enmity between you and the woman, and between your offspring and hers; he will crush your head, and you will strike his heel." (Genesis 3:14–15)*

Pay attention to the last sentence in particular. This is considered to be the first prophetic word concerning Jesus, who would come and break the power of the enemy who had gotten between Man and God. It was a symbolic way of stating that Jesus would destroy Satan, but not before Satan inflicted a little damage of his own.[12]

Verse fourteen is interesting as well. How many snakes do you know that eat dust? If you peek ahead to verse nineteen, you will find out why God chose these particular words: "For dust you are and to dust you will return." Dust in Scripture refers to man's flesh, most often in the context of our sinful nature. That is where the snake—Satan—strikes us, in our flesh, our pride, greed, lust, and fear (cf. Romans 7—8).

Adam and Eve could no longer hear what God had to say to them. They did not trust him; they feared him. But this problem did not hinder God from communicating. It just meant he had to use a new language that circumvented Adam and Eve's false paradigm.

Unfortunately, Adam and Eve passed down this inability to hear God to their offspring. We are also born looking at life through a black sheet of glass. Like Adam and Eve, we tend to view God as an enemy rather than a friend. We fear him; we try to hide from him. When God asks for information, we blame-shift. Satan's fangs are still sunk deep into our flesh. Therefore, as he did with Adam and Eve, God continues to use a different language to speak to us.

> *In the last days, God says, I will pour out my Spirit on all people. Your sons and daughters will prophecy, your young men will have visions, your old men will dream dreams.*
>
> *Even on my servants, both men and women, I will pour out my Spirit in those days, and they will prophecy, I will show wonders in the heavens above and signs on the earth below. (Acts 2:17–19)*

God uses the language of the prophet, the language of divine symbolism. He uses this language to speak to us through dreams and visions and, as I argue in this book, through the everyday events of life. To help us get past our false paradigms, to help us hear and see properly, God uses a language that must not only be heard; it must be walked out in relationship with him.

Now that we've seen where it all started, in the next chapter we will do a brief survey of the Bible to see how God's use of symbolic language developed and grew from the Garden of Eden until the time of Christ and beyond.

[1] "Stunned Japanese Offer Sympathy as Some are Struck by Symbolism," *New York Times,* January 9, 1992, p. A8.

[2] Schlossstein, Steven. *The End of the American Century.* New York: Congdon & Weed 1989. p. 7.

[3] http://www.vision-uk.org/jrn10404/pharoah.html.

[4] John James Davis, *Moses and the Gods of Egypt.* (Grand Rapids: Baker Publishing Group, 1971), p. 94.

[5] *Moses and the Gods of Egypt*, p. 94.

[6] William Smith, *OT History: From Creation to the Return of the Jews from Captivity.* (New York: Harper, 1880), p. 160.

[7] http://www.khouse.org/articles/2000/263.

[8] *Moses and the Gods of Egypt,* p. 126.

[9] Before Jesus could defeat Satan, he first had to suffer and die at the hands of Man.

Chapter Three

SYMBOLIC LANGUAGE IN THE BIBLE

Moriah, Canaan – *circa 1,500* BC – *It is being reported that Abraham, a nomadic herdsman of some repute, has taken his only son Isaac into the wilderness, supposedly to sacrifice him to his God. Has he gone crazy or just senile? Search parties have been dispatched.*

Qantir, Egypt – *circa 1,280* BC – *Today, Jews everywhere slaughtered their lambs believing that smearing the lambs' blood on their doorposts would protect them from the Angel of Death, which they believe is about to be loosed upon the nation. We will keep you posted as events unfold. Film at eleven.*

Nineveh, Assyria – *circa 760* BC – *Witnesses confirm that a wild looking man has been going around town prophesying the city's imminent destruction. His pale, slimy appearance is said to be the result of spending three nights in a whale's belly before being vomited up on shore. Interview to follow.*

Recognize any of these "news bytes"? Rewriting such biblical events like they might appear today on CNN is fun, but it also helps us imagine how people might have regarded them at the time. We all have the advantage of viewing these incidents through the lens of history. We know how the story ended. But for the people involved, events were unfolding in "real time," and they had no idea how things would turn out. I often wonder: Did the average person realize that God was speaking to them through these events, foreshadowing what was to come? Did they see that the Great Author was about to unfold yet another chapter in the story of his dealings with their nation? I believe some of them did, because the Jewish mind in particular allowed for God to speak symbolically through the affairs of the day. But many more people would have probably responded the same way most of us do today. They may have noted the odd occurrences but written them off as merely an anomaly, a strange albeit highly symbolic coincidence.

Most of us miss what God is saying for the same reason many people back then missed it. We may believe God spoke through symbolic events in the past, but we have a difficult time believing he is doing the same thing today. We tend to believe the Great Author put away his pen long ago, when in fact he is actually the most active "blogger" in the world—offering an ongoing commentary on everything and anything going on in the world today. The goal of this book is to help you undergo a paradigm shift so you are able to look beyond mere facts and figures and see what God is saying through the events unfolding all around you. I want to help you develop a paradigm that will allow you to see that God is still in control of the destiny of humankind, and to help you stand in awe once again as you watch the Great Author write his masterpiece.

It will be much easier for you to accept the fact that God still speaks through current events, like George Bush's troubled visit to Japan, if you first see how God spoke through events in the Bible. As you saw with the story of the plagues, the Bible contains numerous examples of how God used foreshadowing or prophetic symbolism to communicate his intentions to humankind. One of my favorites? How about the way God foreshadowed Jesus through the Passover lamb? In AD 2005, this idea makes perfect sense. But what about in the time of Moses, when the first Passover Feast took place?

As cited in the news byte above, God instructed the Jews, who were living as slaves in Egypt, to kill a lamb and spread its blood on their doorposts. This was done so the Angel of Death would not strike down their firstborn sons when he came to kill the firstborn sons of the Egyptians. In a very literal sense, the people were saved by the blood of the lamb, symbolizing what the blood of Christ, also known as "the Lamb of God," (cf. John 1:29) would later do for us. Today, we readily accept the symbolism of Christ as the Lamb of God. But in Jesus' time, the connection was not quite so apparent. People had to pay attention to the signs. Even the disciples didn't get it at first, despite the fact that Jesus explained it to them during the last supper (cf. Matthew 26:26–29) and on the road to Emmaus (Luke 24:13–32). He went through the entire Scriptures (what we now call the Old Testament) and pointed out all of the events that foreshadowed the story God had been writing throughout the ages—the story of his Son. It truly is the greatest story ever told, given in little hints and foreshadowed puzzle pieces for the people of God to figure out along the way.

One important puzzle piece was the story of Abraham and his only son, Isaac. In this story, God asked Abraham to offer Isaac as a human sacrifice. Abraham obeyed, but just before he plunged the knife into Isaac's chest, God intervened and supplied a ram for the sacrifice instead (Genesis 22:13). It turns out that God was merely testing Abraham's faith, seeing if he would take the most precious thing he possessed—his son—and give him to God.

This story is probably quite familiar to you. But can you begin to see the prophetic foreshadowing behind this event? It's fairly simple, I agree. Abraham's willingness to offer up his only son to God foreshadowed how God would sacrifice his only Son Jesus to atone for our sins.

Going to our third news byte above, the story of Jonah foreshadowed yet another aspect of Christ's story—his death and resurrection. Just as Jonah spent three days in the whale's belly before emerging and prophesying to the people of Ninevah so they might be saved, Jesus would also spend three days in death's grip before emerging from the tomb victorious over sin and death. Jesus did not wait until his walk along the road to Emmaus to connect the dots between these two events, either. He stated the connection clearly when the Pharisees and Sadducees came to him asking for a sign to verify that he had come from God. But even though Jesus spoke clearly, no one seemed to understand what he was saying (cf. Matthew 16:4; Luke 11:29).

Going Deeper

Think of the drawings from chapter one again. Remember the feelings of joy and surprise when you were finally able to see another picture hidden right under your nose? All you needed was a new set of eyes, as it were. I have already given you a taste of what that sort of paradigm shift feels like with a few Bible stories. Now let's take a closer look at a number of other Bible stories that you have probably heard about all of your life. Until now, you have probably seen only one picture in such events. However, as we did with the plagues, let's see if we can't find a deeper picture within each one as well.

King Saul and Samuel

In 1 Samuel 15:27–29, Samuel announced that God had just rejected Saul as king, because Saul had disobeyed the Lord's command by allowing his soldiers to keep some of the Amalekites' animals as plunder. In anguish, Saul confessed his guilt and begged for forgiveness. But Samuel said to him, "I will not go back with you. You have rejected the word of the Lord, and the Lord has rejected you as king over Israel" (1 Samuel 15:24–25).

Enter prophetic foreshadowing as the Great Writer makes his point clear… "As Samuel turned to leave, Saul caught hold of the edge of his robe and it tore." Looking down, Samuel recognized this as a sign—the Great Author's foreshadowing of the future—and he interpreted it immediately for Saul: "The Lord has torn the kingdom of Israel from you today and has given it to one of your neighbors—to one better than you" (1 Samuel 15:27).

Through his actions, Saul unwittingly foretold his own doom. It took an insightful man like Samuel to see beyond a seemingly insignificant event—the tearing of his robe—and spot the hand of God at work. Realizing there is no division between the physical realm and the spiritual realm, Samuel saw what happened and gave the event its proper meaning.

Isaiah and Hezekiah

Another great example of foreshadowing is found in 2 Kings 20:12–17. King Hezekiah, who had a terminal illness, cried out to the Lord and was healed. The King of Babylon heard of Hezekiah's recovery and sent out messengers bearing letters and a gift. Hezekiah received the messengers and showed them everything in his palace—all of his gold, silver, treasures, his storehouses, and his armory. There was nothing in his palace he did not show them.

> *Then Isaiah the prophet went to King Hezekiah and asked, "What did those men say and where did they come from?"*
>
> *"From a distant land." Hezekiah replied. "They came from Babylon."*
>
> *The prophet asked, "What did they see in your palace?"* *(2 Kings 20:12–15)*

Why do you think Isaiah asked these questions? What was he looking for? Remember: In Isaiah's mind, there was no distinction between the physical realm and the spiritual realm. That's right! Isaiah was looking for divine foreshadowing.

Consider King Hezekiah's response to Isaiah's query: "'They saw everything in my palace,' Hezekiah said. 'There is nothing among my treasures that I did not show them.'" (2 Kings 20:15b). Isaiah listened to the king's response and interpreted what the Great Author had just written with the tool of foreshadowing. Then he made his reply.

> *"Hear the word of the Lord: The time will surely come when everything in your palace, and all that your fathers have stored*

IF THIS WERE A DREAM, WHAT WOULD IT MEAN?

until this day, will be carried off to Babylon. Nothing will be left, says the Lord." (Isaiah 20:16–17)

Isaiah put a spiritual interpretation on an apparently ordinary physical event. As surely as Hezekiah had shown the Babylonians everything he possessed, soon the Babylonians would come to possess everything they had seen. Unwittingly, Hezekiah had foreshadowed the downfall of his kingdom. It took a prophet like Isaiah, a man "tuned in" to God's symbolic language, to point this out.

It is interesting to note the time lapse between the prophetic sign and its fulfillment in these last two examples. Neither foreshadowed event happened right away. Saul was still king for years afterwards, and, in the case of Hezekiah, Israel was not defeated by the Babylonians for another 200 years. The word of the Lord proved true, but the timing of that word was another factor altogether. We will discuss the matter of timing at length in a later chapter.

Elisha and Jehoash

Now Elisha was suffering from the illness from which he died. Jehoash went down to see him and wept over him. "My father! My father!" He cried. "The chariots and horsemen of Israel!"

Elisha said, "Get a bow and some arrows," and he did so.

"Take the bow in your hands," he said to the king of Israel. When he had taken it, Elisha put his hands on the king's hands.

"Open the east window," he said, and he opened it. "Shoot!" Elisha said, and he shot. "The Lord's arrow of victory over Aram!" Elisha declared. "You will completely destroy the Arameans at Aphek."

Then he said, "Take the arrows," and the king took them, "Strike the ground." He struck it three times and stopped. The man of God was angry with him and said, "you should have struck the ground five or six times; then you would have defeated

Aram and completely destroyed it. But now you will only defeat it three times."

Elisha died and was buried. (2 Kings 13:15–18)

The first question that comes to mind when I read this passage is: Why did Elisha get angry with Jehoash for striking the ground only three times? Should the king have known how many times to strike the ground? Elisha seemed to think so. He expected the king to have some idea about the interconnectedness between physical events and prophetic signs, and this was his way of testing that knowledge. Elisha was angry with the king, because he demonstrated a lack of knowledge about the ways of God. This ignorance would lead eventually to Israel's destruction.

Ezekiel

Around 587 BC, the armies of Babylon surrounded Jerusalem. Jeremiah was in Jerusalem warning the people to give themselves up without a fight, and Ezekiel was in captivity in Babylon telling the people that God had handed Jerusalem over to the Babylonians. There would be no escape. The problem was, the people did not believe God would give Jerusalem over to the Babylonians.

Do not trust in deceptive words and say, "This is the temple of the Lord, the temple of the Lord, the temple of the Lord!" (Jeremiah 7:4)

Will you steal and murder, commit adultery and perjury, burn incense to Baal and follow other gods you have not known, and then come and stand before me in this house [the temple] which bears my name, and say, "We are safe"—safe to do all these detestable things? (Jeremiah 7:9–10)

The children of Israel were confused. They believed that as long as they continued to go to God's temple, they were safe. They could sin and kill and do whatever they wanted, just as long as the temple remained.

Why did they believe this? They thought God lived in the temple. Consequently, Jerusalem could never fall to the Babylonians. God would never allow his home to be taken over by such pagans, and he would never abandon his home either. That is a basic summary of the Jewish paradigm of that day. There was just one problem: It was also a false paradigm.

God had been warning the Jews for some time that this false paradigm was going to get them all killed. Contrary to what they believed, they could not go on sinning, just because they were the chosen people, and expect to get away with it. If anything, God demanded a higher standard from them. God tried to warn them by explaining specifically what would happen if they didn't give up their sinful ways. But they couldn't hear him anymore. So God took another approach: symbolic language. Specifically, he got Ezekiel to begin acting out some signs that described what would happen to the Jews if they did not turn from their sin.

> *Therefore, son of man, pack your belongings for exile in the daytime, as they watch, set out and go from where you are to another place. Perhaps they will understand, though they are a rebellious house. (Ezekiel 12:3)*

When the people asked Ezekiel what this was all about, God instructed Ezekiel to tell them: "I am a sign to you. As I have done, so it will be done to them [the people in Jerusalem]. They will go into exile as captives" (Ezekiel 12:11). God used symbolic language to make the Jews think, to draw them into a state of pondering. Here are a few other examples of how God did this through Ezekiel:

- Siege of Jerusalem acted out with a model (Ezekiel 4:1)
- Laying on his side, symbolizing bearing the sins of Israel and Judah (Ezekiel 4:4)
- Using a sword as a razor (Ezekiel 5:1)
- Exile symbolized (Ezekiel 12:1)
- The cooking pot (Ezekiel 24:1)

60

Despite Ezekiel's best efforts, the people were still unwilling to listen, and, eventually, the things God predicted came to pass.

The Three Gifts

Here's a Bible quiz for you. See if you can get the first part correct: When the Magi came to visit Jesus, what did they bring as gifts? (Hint: Check out Matthew 2:11.) That's right: gold, frankincense, and myrrh. Now here's the difficult part: Why do you think they chose these particular gifts? These gifts were signs, heavenly language, symbols that revealed Jesus' identity and mission. This becomes clear when the signs are interpreted:

- Gold: symbolized royalty, kingship
- Frankincense: This was burned in the temple, implying that this baby would be a priest.
- Myrrh: This was used for embalming at burial, prefiguring Christ's death.

You may have known about these gifts for years, but I'll bet you never realized they were all prophetic signs foreshadowing who Jesus was and what he would do. That's the fun of learning about symbolic language. The old becomes new again, the familiar, fascinating.

The Wedding Feast

Turning water into wine at the wedding feast in Cana was the first miraculous sign Jesus performed. For the first time, he revealed his glory, and his disciples put their faith in him (John 2:11). Remember: the word "sign" is used in Scripture to refer to events the Great Author uses to foreshadow what he is about to do on earth. So what was the sign of Jesus turning water into wine all about? What did it foreshadow? Many believe it is symbolic of the great wedding that is to come between the Bridegroom (Jesus) and his Bride (the Church). The water stands for the Old Covenant, which was replaced by the New Covenant—the wine! With this single act, Jesus foreshadowed the New Covenant, his death (the wine would later become a symbol for his blood), and the eventual wedding between him and his Church (cf. Revelation 19:6–9). Foreshadowing at its best!

A Bad Hair Day for Jesus?

Early in the morning, as he was on his way back to the city, [Jesus] was hungry.

Seeing a fig tree by the road, he went up to it, but found nothing on it except leaves. Then he said to it, "May you never bear fruit again!" Immediately the tree withered.

When the disciples saw this, they were amazed. "How did the fig tree wither so quickly?" they asked.

Jesus replied, "I tell you the truth, if you have faith and do not doubt, not only can you do what was done to the fig tree, but also you can say to this mountain, 'Go, throw yourself into the sea,' and it will be done.

If you believe, you will receive whatever you ask for in prayer."
(Matthew 21:18–22)

Have you ever wondered about this story? Was Jesus just having a bad hair day? Or was something else going on here, a picture within the picture? I certainly think so. All it takes is a bit of research. For example, the fig tree was the national symbol of Israel, just as the eagle is the symbol of America. If you ask an American what an eagle symbolizes, he or she will quickly respond with words like "power," "superiority," and "dignity." If you asked a Jew of that time what a fig tree symbolized, you would get a similarly quick response; only he or she would likely use words such as "provision," "bounty," and "abundance." Figs were a staple food in the region, so an abundance of fruitful fig trees became symbolic of Israel's long-term peace and prosperity.

A bit of context is also helpful: Jesus had just entered Jerusalem riding on a donkey, and all the people were praising him. From here, Jesus proceeded to the temple to take a look around. As you may remember, he didn't like what he saw (Matthew 21:12–13). Immediately following his cleansing of the temple, he went out to Bethany to spend the night (Matthew 21:17). The cursing of the fig tree happened the next morning on his way back into Jerusalem. When he arrived there, he went straight to the temple to confront the Pharisees.

Interestingly, Mark's account of this incident reveals that figs were not even in season yet. What are the odds that Jesus, who had grown up around fig trees all of his life, would not have known that? I am no farmer, but having been around raspberry bushes my entire life (I live in the "raspberry capital of Canada"), I know enough to tell you that you will not find leaves on the bushes until April, and you will not find any fruit until the end of June. Jesus was not a farmer either, but I am certain he was no less observant than me. So if ignorance isn't the answer, let's look a little deeper.

After the fig tree incident, Jesus proceeded into the temple, where he was questioned by the chief priests and elders of the people (Matthew 21:23). They wanted to know by whose authority he was acting. Jesus replied with a series of parables, the last one being about a vineyard, the tenant of which killed the servants whom the owner sent to collect his rent. In the end, they even killed the landowner's son so they could steal his inheritance. Through this parable, Jesus implied that it was people like the Pharisees who had killed the prophets God sent to them, and now they would kill Jesus as well. As if that wasn't enough, Jesus made this statement regarding the Pharisees: "Therefore, I tell you that the kingdom of God will be taken away from you and given to a people who will produce fruit" (Matthew 21:43).

The fig tree, representing Israel, did not bear any fruit. Then, that same morning, Jesus told the Pharisees that the Kingdom of God would be taken away from the Jews and given to someone else, because the Jews were not bearing any fruit. Clearly, his cursing of the fig tree—the national symbol of Israel—was meant to foreshadow events to come: the destruction of Jerusalem and the Jewish state and the beginning of the Gentile church. Even though this sounds harsh, Jesus did not do this out of hatred but out of love. As Jesus states,

"O Jerusalem, Jerusalem, you who kill the prophets and stone those sent to you, how often I have longed to gather your children together, as a hen gathers her chicks under her wings, but you were not willing! Look, your house is left to you desolate. I tell you the truth, you will not see me again until you say, 'Blessed is He who comes in the name of the Lord" (Matthew 23:37–39).

A Net Full Of Fish

The calling of the disciples through the miraculous catch of fish is another good example of how Jesus used physical events to foreshadow things to come. Luke 5 records how, in the midst of teaching the people, Jesus got into Peter's boat and asked him to pull a little ways from shore so he could address the entire crowd from a distance.

When he was finished teaching, Jesus told Peter to put out into deep water and let down his nets. Peter responded that he and his partners, James and John, had been fishing all night but had caught nothing. However, because Jesus requested it, they would do it.

Lo and behold, when they let down their net, they caught so many fish that their net began to break! Peter fell on his knees in astonishment. He had never seen anything like it! To work all night and catch nothing, and then, in one swoop of the net, to catch so many fish the net began to tear—Whoever heard of such a thing? Suddenly, Peter, James and John were a little freaked out, but Jesus reassured them, saying, "'Don't be afraid; from now on you will catch men.' So they pulled their boats up on shore, left everything and followed him" (Luke 5:10–11).

Jesus certainly knew how to capture his future disciples' attention. He did not waste any time making a direct connection between the physical event and the deeper meaning it symbolized either. "As you caught fish, so now you will catch men." But is there something more here?

After Jesus' death, Peter despaired of ever doing anything for the Lord again. He decided he might as well go back to doing what he had always done—fishing. Some of the other disciples joined him. Once again, they were out all night fishing and caught nothing.

The next morning, Jesus appeared on the shore and told them to throw their net over the other side of the boat. Once again, they hauled in a huge load of fish. In fact, this catch was so big they had to drag the net onto shore. Afterwards, Jesus ate with them. Then, in a now famous passage, Jesus reinstated Peter, asking him to "Follow me!" (John 21:19)

What just happened here? Jesus gave the disciples the same sign of commissioning he had given them at the start: a miraculous catch of fish. Through this act, Jesus showed his disciples that he had forgiven them for abandoning him. Jesus also used this incident to call the disciples back into ministry. He did this by reenacting the glorious day of their first adventure with him, showing the disciples that things would be just like the old days, only better! But Jesus did not stop there.

Examining the Net a Little Closer

Let's use our new awareness of divine foreshadowing to see if we can find a deeper meaning to these events than our previous paradigm allowed.

Back when Jesus first called the disciples, he said that just as they caught fish, now they would catch men. So if the fish in that scenario symbolized people, then the net must have symbolized the disciples. Just as Man used nets to catch fish, God would use the disciples to catch men.

Remember how the net tore during the first miraculous catch? The net could not take the strain. In the same way, when Jesus died, the same thing happened to the disciples, the disciples could not take the strain. Unable to accept that Jesus had died, the disciples abandoned Jesus and lost their catch of men for the Kingdom of God. Now jump ahead to the recommisioning. Jesus used the same sign again but with one significant difference: "Simon Peter climbed aboard and dragged the net ashore. It was full of large fish, 153, but even with so many *the net was not torn*" (John 21:11). The net, which represented the disciples, failed the first time, and so did the disciples. But after the second catch of fish, the net did not break, signifying that the disciples would not break either. They would bring thousands of people into the Kingdom of God, a miraculous catch!

But one question remains: What particular flaw in the disciples' character did the tear in the net portray? What false paradigm did it reveal? To arrive at an answer, we need to know what aspect of the disciples' character the Lord was dealing with. What issue showed itself at the beginning of his relationship with them and was only finally resolved at the time of the second catch? The crux of the matter can be summed up as follows:

> *But we have this treasure in jars of clay to show that this all surpassing power is from God and not from us.*
>
> *We always carry around in our body the death of Jesus, so the life of Jesus may also be revealed on our body. (2 Corinthians 4:7,10)*
>
> *For to be sure he was crucified in weakness, yet he lives by God's power. Likewise, we are weak in him, yet by God's power we will live with him to serve you. (2 Corinthians 13:4)*

Before the crucifixion, the disciples—particularly Peter—did not realize that they were merely fragile, earthen vessels. Remember: One of the most popular topics of discussion among the disciples concerned which one of them would be the greatest in God's kingdom (cf. Matthew 18:1; Mark 9:33, 10:35; Luke 22:24). The disciples thought Jesus was going to set up an earthly kingdom, and they wanted to be first in line to help him rule it (cf. Acts 1:6; Mark 10:35). In short, they suffered from pride.

Three disciples in particular who suffered from this affliction were James, his brother John, and Peter. Jesus spent a good deal of time with these three men, even taking them up the mountain when he was transfigured (Matthew 17). Jesus called James and John the "Sons of Thunder," possibly in reference to James and John wanting to call down fire from heaven to destroy a Samaritan village (Luke 9:54). These guys did not display a lot of humility or compassion.

Peter was often the spokesman for the disciples. In this role, he was often presumptuous. Here are a few examples of Peter's confidence in his own convictions:

- Peter's attempt to walk on water (Matthew 14:28)
- Peter tells Jesus that he will surely not die (Matt 16:22)
- Peter offers to build shelters for Elijah, Moses, and Jesus during the transfiguration (Matt 17:4)
- Peter wants to know what's in it for the disciples if they follow Jesus (Matthew 19:27)
- Peter declares he will never fall away (Matt 26:23)
- Peter refuses to allow Jesus to wash his feet (John 13:8)
- Peter cuts off the ear of the High Priest's servant (John 18: 10)

Peter was a man who was confident of his earthly abilities. As such, he was the epitome of the rest of the disciples, who were all confident in their own strength. However, Jesus did not choose these men for their strength. He chose them for their weakness. As Paul declared, when we are weak, then we are strong (2 Corinthians 12:10). Thus, before they could be of any use to Jesus, the disciples had to discover how weak they were. They could not usher in the Kingdom of God by their own strength. This could only be done through the power of the Holy Spirit. But before the disciples could receive the Holy Spirit, they needed to discover how much they needed him.

The Beginning of the End

Over the nearly three years that Jesus and the disciples spent together, Jesus taught them a lot of things. But as Jesus' time on earth drew to a close, the issue of pride remained. In Luke 22, we find the story of the Last Supper, an intimate moment between Jesus and his disciples right before his arrest and execution. After the meal was served, an amazing thing happened: Once again, the disciples began arguing about who was the greatest among them! Jesus responded to this argument by telling the disciples that it is the Gentiles that flaunt their authority over one another. The disciples were not to be like that. Instead, the greatest among them was the one who served the others. Jesus ended this discussion by turning to Peter and saying, "Simon, Simon, Satan has asked to sift you [all of the disciples] like wheat. But I have prayed for you, Simon, that your faith may not fail. And when you have turned back, strengthen your brothers" (Luke 22:31).

Through their association with Jesus, the disciples had come to believe that they were "hot stuff." Jesus was warning them that Satan would exploit this hubris to his advantage. After all, pride is Satan's domain. Why wouldn't he walk through this door if the disciples were holding it open for him? Satan would scatter the disciples, humiliating them by exposing their lack of character in the face of persecution. He would make a mockery of their human strength. Yet the Lord had a purpose in all of this: Revealing their human weakness was the only way the disciples could see their need for his divine power. It was the only way to bring about a paradigm shift.

Peter still didn't get it. He believed that his own zeal would be enough in the moment of truth, and he had enough gall to look Jesus in the face and tell him so. "But he [Peter] replied, "Lord, I am ready to go with you to prison and to death" (Luke 22:33). At this point, the Lord reveals the final sign that will signal the conclusion of his dealings with the disciples in the area of pride: "Jesus answered, 'I tell you, Peter, before the rooster crows today, you will deny three times that you know me'" (Luke 22:34).

The following sequence of events is a blur, including Jesus' arrest and trial. Let's pick up the narrative at Luke 22:59:

> *About an hour later another asserted, "Certainly this fellow was with him, for he is a Galilean."*
>
> *Peter replied, "Man, I don't know what you are talking about!" Just as he was speaking, the rooster crowed. The Lord turned and looked straight at Peter. Then Peter remembered the word the Lord had spoken to him: "Before the rooster crows today, you will disown me three times." And he went outside and wept bitterly. (Luke 22:59–62)*

When the rooster crowed, Jesus' effort to expose Peter's pride was complete. For the first time in his life, Peter could see himself for what he was: a man in need of a savior, a man who could not usher in the Kingdom of God by his own strength, a man who would deny his best friend to save his own skin.

The weakness in the net had been revealed. Just as the net was not strong enough to hold the fish, neither were the disciples strong enough to follow the Lord in their own strength. Just as the net at the re-commissioning in John 21 needed the power of God to hold it together, so the disciples needed the power of the Holy Spirit to keep them together as they fulfilled the mission Christ set before them.

Why the Rooster?

As we learned in our discussion of the plagues, God does not choose prophetic signs at random. When God gives a physical sign, it always lines up with the story he has been telling. Why the rooster? Roosters symbolize pride. Our colloquialisms still reflect this association today. "He sure is a cocky fellow," we say, or "He is all puffed up like a rooster." In Jesus' time, the association was no different. The last sign fit with what the Lord was dealing with in the disciples' lives. They were cocky. Just as a rooster tries to dominate the hen house, so the disciples had tried to dominate each other. They also hoped to be rulers in Jesus' kingdom so they could dominate everyone. The rooster illustrated this character flaw perfectly.

Think back to Jesus' discussion with the disciples at the Last Supper. He had rebuked them for lording their authority over one another. He even told Peter to his face that he, Peter, would turn away, but Peter denied it. The disciples' reliance on their own strength could be hidden no longer. Their false paradigm had been exposed. The "pride chapter" of the disciples' lives was now over, meaning that the next chapter in the Great Author's work—the re-instatement of the disciples—could begin. Jesus was all set to fire the starting pistol once again. The disciples were about to make another miraculous catch; but this time the net would not break, and neither would they.

Take a Step Backward

These are but a few examples of foreshadowing in the Bible. I could write an entire book on such biblical examples alone. However, I hope this brief survey gives you enough confidence to see that God does use such symbolic events to foretell what he is going to do on earth, and that he has been doing so for thousands of years. We will study more biblical stories later on.

For now, I would like to restate what I said at the outset of this chapter: As we examine these stories from the Bible, it is easy to see what these signs foreshadowed, because we have the entire story in front of us. However, when we are seeking to understand a sign the Lord is giving us today, we don't have the advantage of hindsight to guide us. All we have is our limited, "in the moment" point of view. We are forced to follow events as they unfold, interpreting them on the fly and trusting that they will make sense in the end. Therefore, we must become an observant people—a people who understand the Lord's heart and his ways. We need to develop a paradigm that allows us to look beyond the surface, to catch the Great Writer in the act of writing, to follow him to the journey's end.

To show you how I came to believe this, in the next chapter I would now like to share my own initial encounter with God's symbolic language and how it transformed my way of viewing the world.

Chapter Four

LEARNING THINGS THE HARD WAY...

I learned to understand God's symbolic language not because I wanted to but because I had to. My survival depended on it, both mentally and physically.

At the time, I was pastoring a youth church called God Rock, which included some 250 kids. These were not your average kids either. Fifty percent were from broken homes, and many came directly from the streets of Vancouver, BC. Many had been sexually abused. When "normal" people have a bad day, they deal with it by going home and watching TV or loading up on ice cream. For many of the troubled young people I was dealing with, their response to a bad day was to slice their wrists. When one girl who had come out of a hard scene was raped and ended up in the psych ward, I began to lose hope. I wondered if God really cared or if I could help them at all.

Not long afterwards, a famous prophet came to our church for a conference. It was great; the presence of God was really strong. However, at a staff meeting the day before the conference, our head pastor, Gareth[1], shared a strange yet compelling dream that his wife had experienced the night before. In the dream, she was somewhere in the Southern states at night. She saw a woman on a bridge. The woman turned to her and said, "Help me, I'm trapped in Birmingham, Alabama!" She also dreamed there was an earthquake. It felt so real that when she woke up, she checked to see if things were shaking. It didn't make a lot of sense, but suddenly I found myself fighting back tears. What was going on?

That evening, we had our meeting with the prophetic fellow. He told us that as a church, we had a chance to go down in history, either having been used of God in a mighty way or missing it, like Birmingham, Alabama. As it turns out, in 1996 God had granted Birmingham an anointing for regional revival. However, a sin issue amongst church leadership quenched what God was up to. This got our attention! The prophet went on to say that the enemy was going to hit us with everything he had for the next eighteen months, and that we needed to work on intimacy with our spouses and with the Lord.

After that meeting, people wanted out of leadership. But life goes on. You just put the word on the shelf and forget about it. We knew we couldn't let a prophetic word run our lives. If God were in it, surely he would bring it to pass in his own good time.

Two months passed after that ugly prophetic word. Christmas came and went, and things weren't going all that great. I still remember the first God Rock service of the New Year. The heat had been turned off, due to some kind of misunderstanding with another tenant who shared our building, and none of the chairs were set up. If you weren't dressed warmly enough for sledding, you weren't dressed warmly enough to be in the building. No one could stay inside, and there was nowhere to sit if they could. What a way to begin the New Year.

Time went on, and things went from bad to worse. At least three members of our youth congregation were admitted to the psych ward by May. Then, within two weeks, all of the home groups collapsed. One adult leader burned out and had to go on anti-depressants. Another fell heavily into the drug scene. Then a husband/wife leadership team had their van stolen, and their daughter, who was also a leader, had a cancer scare. The list of disasters or near disasters went on and on.

As summer approached, we had a leadership meeting to see who would come back the following September to help. Only three out of twenty-five leaders re-committed. I was devastated. God Rock was dead. I had been training some of these people for years, and now they were walking away. It destroyed me. All of the people I had helped were getting worse, and all of the leaders in whom I had invested were walking away. It was too much for me. I began to crack. The Lord saw that crack in my defenses and walked right through it.

Signs

The next day I went for what felt like the longest drive in history. I took our huge, twelve-person youth tent and went all the way to Long Beach on the west side of Vancouver Island, about a twelve-hour trip. I had not planned to go to the island; I just wanted the remotest place I could find, a place to rest my soul, to lick my wounds. The only way I could get any peace during the drive was by asking God to forgive me for anything that came to mind—judging people, being angry, prideful, etc. I finally stopped driving when I ran out of road on the shore of the Pacific Ocean. I found a place to set up my tent, took a short walk along the beach, and then went to bed.

The next morning I awoke to the strangest noise. It sounded as if a bear was outside my tent. But whatever it was seemed to be flying around my tent. Since I had just woken up, I thought I was imagining things. Then I thought it might be a dragonfly. But it was just too loud! Suddenly, a Bible reference went through my mind: Isaiah 6:6–7. I dug my Bible out of my backpack and looked it up.

> *Then one of the seraphim flew to me, having in his hand a live coal which he had taken with tongs from the alter. And he touched my mouth with it and said: "Behold, this has touched your lips; your iniquity is taken away, and your sin is purged."*

I sat there stunned. I knew God had just given me a clue as to why my life and career were going down the toilet. I knew this had nothing to do with the sins I had been repenting of the night before. This was about something much deeper. It was about how I lived my life on the most fundamental level. But I didn't have a bead on exactly what he was getting at yet.

Not six months earlier, I had a successful ministry. I had grown a youth church from 12 to 250 people in five years. I could reach kids few seemed willing or able to reach. I was speaking at conferences, and we were even planting a youth church in downtown Vancouver. On paper, it looked wonderful. But paper is not the most sturdy of building materials. I sensed that the foundation of my ministry was faulty. It looked sound enough, but I had a feeling that during this season of testing, everything that was based on mixed motives would be burned up. The Lord *is* gracious and compassionate, but when the time comes, he knows how to play hardball as well.

I had worked so hard, and I was proud of what I had accomplished. That is exactly what the Lord was after: my fierce independence, my need to succeed, to prove my worth, to "fix" everyone that came my way. Now I was left holding nothing but ashes. The only glimmer of hope I possessed was the sense that I had been forgiven. But I still didn't know precisely what I had done wrong. Obviously, it was time for a paradigm shift. The picture within the picture was there. But so far, I just couldn't see it.

More Puzzle Pieces, More Questions

God gave me another piece of the puzzle one day as I was out walking on Sumas Prairie. I was telling God how unfair it all was when he gave me a picture of a metal-toothed monster. I hated that picture, but intuitively, I knew it had something to do with how God Rock functioned. That metal-toothed monster represented part of the God Rock structure that should not have been there. But I had no idea what that was.

The next clue arrived while some people were praying for me. I saw myself rolling a huge bolder up a hill. I was straining with all my might. As I looked at the picture, the Lord let me know that he never asked me to roll that boulder up the hill. Take note: I was a leader at God *Rock,* and I was looking at a picture of me straining to push a *boulder.* The symbolism couldn't be much clearer, could it? But I still didn't get it.

Even though God Rock was closing down, we had one ministry trip to Montana to which we were committed. The Sunday before we left, the church was commissioning our team through prayer when I fell to the floor. As I lay there, I heard the Lord speak to me in my mind, as loud as I have ever heard. "I've beaten you," he said. His voice was full of compassion and love, but there was no mistaking the meaning. The demise of God Rock—he was behind it! I still didn't know what this was all about, but I sensed I would get more information as the trip began.

Montana

We had driven for twelve hours. There were twenty of us altogether, split between four vehicles. We had just crossed into Montana, and everyone wanted to make a pit stop. I found the nearest gas station and pulled over. It turns out that nearly every gas station in Montana is also half casino, which didn't appeal to me at all. I told the others I would meet them at the next rest stop. Then I got into my van with a few others and left. This was not the best thing for a leader to do, but I was not in the best frame of mind, and there were others who could watch the troops. For some reason, I felt I just had to get to the next rest area.

The trip took longer than expected, about twenty-five minutes. I remember Neil, one of the young adults, asking how much farther it was. Then the Lord told me it was right around the corner. I had enough faith left at that time to say that out loud. Sure enough, we drove around the corner and there it was—a sign that said, "Rest Area." The moment I read it, I felt as if someone had knocked the breath out of me. It was time to pay attention. God was about to add another piece to the puzzle.

Once we stopped, I spotted a huge historical information sign that said "Iron Mountain Mine," or something similar. I felt the Lord urging me to read it, so I walked over for a closer look. In summary, it said that twelve miles from this rest area was the Iron Mountain Mine. In 1897, miners pulled out millions of dollars of ore in one year. However, a law was passed stating that any mine without a secondary escape shaft had to be shut down for safety reasons, so the mine was closed. They tried to start it up again, but to no avail. All that is left today is collapsed tunnels and crumbling foundations.

I was stunned by the information. It seemed to fit my situation perfectly. A tremendous start-up followed by a sudden collapse. What was the Lord saying? That we couldn't start again? It is probably important to note at this point that despite the apparent dissolution of our ministry, we were still planning to start up God Rock again in the fall.

I read the sign over and over, pondering it in my mind. After a while, I came to this conclusion: Just as the mine was built twelve miles outside of the rest area, so was the leadership of God Rock built outside of God's resting place (Psalm 91:1–3). I knew God was referring to leadership, because the number twelve constantly refers to leadership in Scripture: twelve apostles, twelve tribes, twelve gates, twelve thrones, etc. (More on that later.) The foundation of God Rock—its leadership team—had based its ministry on identity, striving, and pride. I knew nothing could be built on such a foundation. It was not safe for us or those we led.

This may seem like a lot of information to glean from one little sign, but it was exactly what I needed to put the previous puzzle pieces together. The image of me struggling with the boulder showed how I was striving to do everything in my own strength. The metal-toothed monster—my concept of ministry at God Rock—was the result of that striving. Now I was beginning to see why I needed forgiveness. I was struggling with a performance mentality, driven to succeed as a way of proving my worth. That desire was undermining everything I did for the Kingdom. I did not know how to find rest in God. I did not know how to receive God's love merely for who I was, rather than what I did.

Even with what had just happened, I knew I could still be wrong. I was willing to crumple up my hypothesis and throw it away. If this was God, I was confident that still more clues would be forthcoming. I did not have to wait long.

"Meet Me In the Fields..."

Montana is a beautiful state with wide-open prairie on both sides of the Rockies. The mountains and streams are phenomenal, great places to hear the Lord, think, and collect your thoughts. One day, I woke up with a picture of the rolling prairie in my mind. Again, I heard the Lord speak so loudly his voice could have been audible. "Come out into the fields," he said. "I want to meet with you today."

That afternoon, I drove out into the prairie and sat on a rock. I waited. Nothing. I waited longer. Still nothing. Oh well. Maybe I would come back in the evening and see what, if anything, would happen then.

I went to the next event, which happened to be a barbeque at the church. This church was not your typical set-up. Before it was a church, it was a driving range. The church had a vast open space behind it surrounded by wheat fields. I ate some food and played some hacky-sack until a fellow walked up to me and said he wanted to talk. He was in his late forties, had been a Ranger in the Vietnam War and, although I did not know it at the time, had a prophetic ministry to the people of the area. He said he had a word for me. I listened politely, not knowing what to think. This is what he said: "I saw a picture of you surfing a set of waves. You were in between sets, and a bigger set was about to come in. I saw that you were caught between sets of waves in the rip tide. You were paddling and paddling to get out. The Lord said that *you are striving. You are outside of his area of rest, and if you don't stop right now, it's going to get worse!*"

Immediately, my mind went back to what I had read about the Iron Mountain Mine. Now I had a lot of questions.

"Let's go for a walk in the fields," he said. "I meet God there." Exactly what the Lord had spoken to me about in my room that morning! It was at that point that I fell to the ground weeping.

Out there amongst the waving wheat, we talked about a lot of things, but especially about intimacy with God and how anything built outside of his rest would not stand. We talked about the "trysting place," an old-fashioned term used to describe where lovers would meet. Once again, I sensed the big picture of what God was doing become slightly clearer. I was beginning to understand what he was after: pure relationship based on love and intimacy. He did not want me to work for him but to be in relationship with him. One of the last things my new friend said was that he believed my false paradigm was based on things that had happened to me while growing up. They were fear-based, but God was going to uproot those issues and replant me in him. That sounded great. Little did I realize how painful transplanting could be.

Waiting For the Quick Fix

Back at home; I waited for more information from the Lord regarding what to do next. I went back walking on Sumas Prairie again, talking to the Lord and trying to understand. I looked up at Sumas Mountain. On the top I could see the radio tower. The sun had just broken through the clouds, making the tower shine and sparkle. I felt the Lord tell me to go up there. Usually, I would have questioned whether the voice was from God. But the way I had been hearing the Lord lately, I knew I could not ignore it.

As I started up the trail that led to the tower, I was singing to the Lord. I felt like this was it. The period of trial was over! God had given me the information I needed, and this was going to be the end of the journey. Things would finally go back to normal. Hallelujah!

Suddenly, the singing stopped. I had arrived at a clear cut, a bald patch of forest where every tree had been cut down. I was standing at the point where two overgrown logging roads met. The path before me was gone; there was no way to reach the tower from where I was. My eyes searched the trees, looking for some sign of the path. Then it began to rain. I raised my head to heaven and shouted at the top of my lungs, "You can't get there from here!"

Furious, I began to descend the way I had come. A verse went through my mind at that point, something about following the ancient paths. I knew it was in Jeremiah somewhere. But I was too angry to care, and I told God so. "How dare you do this to me? I trusted you! I can't get there from here!"

I Can't Get There From Here.

Out of my mouth came the very truth I needed to hear but was unable to comprehend. That was exactly what this little hike was supposed to teach me. Once again, the physical was speaking of the invisible. I thought I had it all figured out. On the way up the mountain, I had interpreted the radio tower as God communicating. All I had to do was get there to receive the message. I was partly right, but God had something slightly different in mind. His point was that the way I was doing life, the path I was following, could not bring me deeper into his presence. In fact, the path I was following was a dead end. Things needed to change. I needed to learn that my human strength would not be enough to get me to the center of God's will. I needed to learn how to fail.

That night, we had a meeting at church. I arrived despondent. However, I was encouraged when, during worship, I saw a picture in my mind of a First Nations person parting the trees and revealing a hidden path. Afterwards, a few people prayed for me, and a couple of them also had a picture of someone parting the trees to reveal a hidden path.

The next morning, my friend Diane came over. God had given her a verse during the night. It was Jeremiah 6:16: "Stand at the crossroads and look; ask for the ancient paths, ask where the good way is, and walk in it, and you will find rest for your souls." I was flabbergasted. It was the same verse I had received while coming down the mountain but had not bothered to look it up. I realized this was all about finding rest again, just like the Lord had spoken of in Montana. Incredible! Once again, God used a physical act—my hike up the mountain—to produce faith and awe in me. Amazing!

The Root Revealed

Later in the week, I had a meeting with Donna, one of my former youth leaders. She had been telling me about a Life Skills course she was taking. One of the things they did in this course was play games that generated emotional responses so participants could learn proper ways of dealing with them. As Donna described one of the games to me, God told me this was exactly what he was doing to me: causing events to happen in my life so he could reveal the state of my heart. God was pushing my buttons! Every time I tried to do something, fix something or get somewhere, I failed, and I got angry!

I must have turned pale at that point, because Donna asked if I was okay. I told her what was going on, and she asked me if I had ever felt that I could never win approval or make the grade. I was about to say "no," when it all came flooding back to me: my relationship with my dad. I had basically frozen him out of my life years ago. He owned a construction company, and I had worked for him for years, but I still could not win his respect or trust. Finally, in anger, I had given up.

This revelation stunned me. I hadn't given any thought to these issues for years. But here they were, still controlling my behavior today. I had tried to earn my father's approval through my efforts, and now the Lord had revealed that I was doing the same thing with him. Worse, I was modeling exactly the same behavior to those I led.

This extra emotional burden was all it took. I began to collapse and slide into burnout. I cried all the time and became emotionally unhinged at the slightest provocation. I could no longer look anyone in the eye or even think coherently. I became the biggest failure in the world, at least in my own eyes.

Healing of the Old Paradigm Begins

It is hard to describe the next season of time. I remember going to see my doctor. When he walked into the office, I started crying. I remember the staff guys at church were going somewhere, and I was supposed to go, too. Something happened about money, a small thing, but I couldn't take it. I ran to my car and drove off. This sort of thing happened constantly.

I went for counseling and realized I had a number of "father issues" to deal with. They were affecting my view of God and how I thought he viewed me. At one point, I even wrote a letter to my dad to tell him how I felt. I had no intention of mailing it. It was more to help me be honest about what I was feeling. Oddly enough, the following day my dad called me! Without me even asking, we talked about all the things that had come between us, the very things I had written about in my letter. It was wonderful. I began to believe the Lord might want to heal me after all.

In my present state, I was next to useless socially and vocationally. I was afraid for my family. Where would the money come from? I remember telling my kids that I would be taking some time off. What would they like to do?

"We want to go to Disneyland!" was the resounding answer.

"Well, let's ask God to provide the money," I said, my heart sinking. So we all prayed and left it with the Lord. The next week, I was going through the mail when I found an envelope that contained a check for $5,000. True to form, I began to cry. Here I was, burnt out, completely useless for anything by Man's standards. I had nothing left for God. Church was a realm of absolute failure and despair to me. And yet, with nothing to give, with no strength or word of praise on my lips, the Lord supplied my needs—and not only my needs but also my children's desires.

I gathered my kids and asked them if they remembered what they had asked God for. "Sure," they said, "Money to go to Disneyland."

"Well," I said, fighting back tears, "Here it is." I'll never forget the looks on their faces. Intimacy with the Father and trust in his goodness began anew for them and for me right then and there. At my lowest point, when I had nothing to give to the church, God or my family, when everything I thought manhood was about was stripped away, I met the Father; and it turned out that all he really wanted was to be my friend.

I wish I could say that school was finally over and life got back to normal, that God's favor returned. But shortly after I returned to work at church, our head pastor went through burnout as well. In fact, it was not long before everyone on staff was seeking more mature brothers and sisters to speak into their lives. I see now that this was God's plan, to teach us not to be so goal-oriented, to stop trying to do things on our own. He wanted us to be relationship-oriented, to find mentors, to slow down, to allow God to be our friend as well as our Lord.

The Continuing Story, the Journey, and the Lesson

It was a beautiful day; a good day for another walk on the prairie, so that is what Gareth and I decided to do. Our prophet friend, the one who had delivered that foreboding word at our church eighteen months earlier, was coming back, and we were all a little nervous. As we walked and talked about the past year, an eagle appeared suddenly and dove toward the creek beside us. Without even making a splash, it pulled a fish out of the water and flew away. Gareth turned and asked me what I thought that meant. I shrugged and said that I guessed we would soon find out.

Our second encounter with the prophetic fellow was tough. He told us we were not out of the woods yet. He also asked us if we had ever heard of "the dark night of the soul," and he brought up the need for us to seek out mentors and deal with father issues. Suffice it to say that after the horrible year we had just gone through, we were all expecting a clean bill of health. To discover that we were still lost in the woods was tough.

Gareth took some time out at a nearby lake to think it all through. When he returned, he told me an interesting story.

"A strange thing happened one day as I was walking along the shore of the lake," he said. "I saw an eagle dive into the lake to get a fish, but it missed. However, it went straight into the water and had to swim ashore. That eagle totally missed it."

I nodded. That image summed up perfectly what the prophetic fellow had said: We had missed it. Eagles are common here in Canada, but I had never seen one catch a fish or heard of one missing a fish and having to swim to shore. To have encountered two eagles like this within a short space of time was not something to be ignored. Once again, I knew that God was giving us puzzle pieces; our paradigm was still out of focus. But we needed more information before the things God was trying to show us would become clear. Thankfully, the additional information was not long in coming.

Power Outage

The sun was streaming through the windows at church one Sunday morning. I was reading my Bible as I listened to Gareth preach. (My wife Kelly was at home with our children, who were sick.) Gareth was talking about the difference between power and authority in the Kingdom of God. Specifically, he described how you had to give up power to gain authority. He used the example of Saul and Samuel.

"Samuel had power; he was a judge of Israel," Gareth said. "He could have tried to hold onto that power in Israel, to retain governmental status. But he gave it up freely, because following the Lord was more important to him. Giving up the power made the people respect and trust him all the more. They saw his integrity, his honesty, and his commitment to God. He had won the right to speak into people's lives."

Gareth continued: "Saul, however, did the opposite. He coveted power and what the people thought of him. It drove him so much that he was willing to kill to keep it. In the end, he had no authority in the people's lives, for they no longer respected him."

And then came the statement I will never forget: "You need to give up power to gain authority." Right then, the bank of lights above the stage went out. Hmm… That's strange, I thought, and noted the incident in my diary.

When I got home, I told my wife about the incident. Just as I reached the part about giving up power for authority, the lights in our house went out, came back on, went out again, and then came back on. Now I was feeling spooked. A power outage twice during the same sentence? What were the odds of that? I knew it was time to pay attention.

Next on the list of church functions was a meeting for home group leaders in the sanctuary. Once again, I was in the midst of talking to the leaders about giving up power to gain authority when the bank of lights above me went out! I looked up at the lights in awe. The odds of something like this happening three times in a row were just this side of insane. But then it happened a fourth time—at an annual business meeting to go over the church's finances.

At this stage in the journey, our church leadership had a good understanding of how performance-driven we were, how we had focused most of our time on doing things *for* God rather than spending time *with* God. But still unanswered was the question of what to do for all of the people who needed home groups and pastoral care while we were in the midst of this massive transition. I knew we had to learn to lay down control, to really listen to each other, to not care how it looked but to follow what we thought God was saying, even if, to the Western eye, it looked foolish. It was a struggle, and there was a lot of miscommunication between us for several months.

This communication problem even extended to my computer. First, it wouldn't connect with the Internet. Then the D drive got erased (twice). The network of computers at the church crashed. The main phone line at church went dead. Even the digital read-out on one of our staff's cars went on the fritz. All of these incidents portrayed exactly what was happening to our church staff at the time.

Finally, I realized God was telling me it was time to leave. The day I resigned, a funny thing happened: The antenna on my car broke off. Even stranger was my reaction—I was ecstatic!

Let me explain: In my experience, God often uses a vehicle to symbolize an individual's ministry or life. We do this as well. For example, if someone asks us how we are doing, we often say things like, "I'm just driving around in circles," or "I'm stuck in the mud," or "I just can't seem to get out of first gear today." I believe God uses these colloquialisms to show us how we are doing and where we are going.

When the prophet came to our church the first time, I did not know these things. It only became obvious as time went on. However, I recalled that both Gareth's and my cars came away from that first conference with huge dents in them. As it turned out, both of us burned out or "crashed" a short while later and had to take some time off.

Back to my antenna: It had been bent for a while, but for some unknown reason, on the day I resigned, it broke right off my car. Why was I ecstatic? Because I realized that if my car represented my ministry, then the antenna represented me. Like the antenna, my job was to "pick up" signals from God, to hear and interpret them for the church. Doing so over the last few years had been a tremendous burden, especially when I had so much trouble finding direction in my own life. Burdens like this are difficult to bear, but they are even harder to let go of, especially when you have been in relationship with so many people for so many years. Even while walking toward my car, I was still worried. What if I was supposed to continue to hear for the body, even in such a wrecked emotional state? The antenna coming off the car gave me peace to know that my decision to leave the church and move on had been the correct one. I still had no idea where I was going, but I knew that I no longer had to hear on behalf of the church. I was released of that duty. It was then that I realized how much watching for physical signs from God had become a part of my daily life. I realized that I had begun to believe that such symbols were as credible as any other form of communication God used with me, and that gave me a wonderful feeling. Yes, God was indeed in control.

Looking Back, Keeping Track

You have now read a bit about how the Great Author began training me to read his signs, events that foreshadow what the Lord is about to do. Losing an old paradigm and gaining a new one is a very costly venture. For me, I had to give up the security I derived from my education, my position as pastor, and my achievements. It was painful, but I knew I would only be able to see life through different eyes if I gave up everything I had built up around me as security. As I said at the outset of this chapter, I learned to understand God's language of symbolism because I had to, not because I wanted to.

Before we leave this story, I would like to recap some of the puzzle pieces or signs God gave to me during this difficult time of transition. Remember: What happened to me was nothing new. The process God used with me was the same process he used with people throughout the Bible. And this is the same process God uses to speak to all of us today—even to you. He only gives us as much information as we can handle. Then, when we are ready, he hands us the next piece.

Timeline of Physical Signs:

1) The vision of the woman on the bridge
2) Gareth's and my vehicles dented at first conference with prophetic minister
3) The heat was off and no chairs were set up at the first God Rock meeting in January
4) My encounter in the tent on the island and Isaiah 6:6–7
5) The vision of the metal-toothed monster
6) The vision of me struggling with the boulder
7) The "Rest Area" sign
8) The "Iron Mountain Mine" sign
9) My hike up Sumas Mountain and the crossroads (Jeremiah 6:16)
10) Computer crashes and car problems
11) The two eagle signs—one diving and catching a fish, the other diving and missing the fish
12) The power going out four times when the phrase "You need to give up power to gain authority" was uttered
13) The crashing of the computer network at the church and the phone line going dead
14) The antenna breaking off my car.

This is not a complete list of events, but taken together with everything else that happened, these puzzle pieces help to complete a picture—a story—written by the Great Author to reveal his heart and purposes for me at the time.

God's Solution to Man's False Paradigm

As I reflect on these events, I find it amazing how my perception of reality was so strong and yet so off track at the same time. I had no idea what the Lord was trying to say to me until several signs had occurred. Even then, I was slow to come to understanding. Like most people, I didn't realize I had a problem. I put in sixty hours per week plus; I spent all my time thinking about ministry, even when I was with my family. I developed a habit of viewing every meeting through the perspective of where that meeting would take my ministry in five months. I worked for a few years at half-time salary, because I believed so strongly that Generation X was going to bring revival to the world. When I was finally able to see that I was wrong, I crashed. All those hours, all those years put into ministry based on a false paradigm—a belief that my effort could produce the Kingdom of God.

Did God try to tell me earlier? I'm sure he did. But I refused to remove the pair of glasses I was currently wearing, the ones that colored and distorted my perception of the world. I saw all of life through the lenses of youth revival. That was all that mattered to me. I would not rest until it happened. That is why God used so much symbolic language to get my attention, because my belief system would not allow me to hear him straight out. Like the disciples, I had to learn things the hard way.

To make things a little easier on you, I would like to pass on a theological framework that I developed throughout this learning process. It takes the form of ten prophetic questions that will help you classify and interpret each puzzle piece as it comes up. Think of the next section as a primer on God's symbolic language. So far, all you've learned is that such a language exists. Now it is time to learn how to read it.

---

[1] Not his real name.

Section II

SEEING LIFE
THROUGH
SYMBOLIC EYES

Chapter Five

LIVING IN THE LAND
OF SYMBOLS

At this point, you may feel as if you have just walked out of your first class in French or Spanish, and your head is spinning as you try to grasp the new lingo. That's okay. Learning any new language takes time. But if you apply yourself, one day you will arrive at that magical moment when you find yourself not only being able to speak the new language, but also thinking and dreaming in it as well! That is exactly what happens when you seek out a new paradigm, a new way of seeing the world.

The good news is; you are already further along the road to thinking and speaking in symbols than you realize. In fact, you probably couldn't communicate without using symbols even if you tried! How do I know this? Just take a look around you. What does an eagle represent to Americans? What do Russians think of when they see an image of a bear? If you live in Canada, what does a red maple leaf signify? Think of your favorite sports team. What sort of image do you associate with it? An animal (Chicago Bulls, BC Lions)? An inanimate object (Detroit Pistons, New York Jets)? A type of person (New England Patriots, Portland Trailblazers) A force of nature (Tampa Bay Lightning, Calgary Flames)? What are these symbols meant to communicate about that team? Power? Speed? Courage?

What about symbolic numbers? "We're number one!" is something you will hear chanted at sports events. Then there's "She's a real ten!" Or "Give me five." Do you know of any office buildings that do not have a 13ᵗʰ floor? Actually, there are quite a few.

Then there are symbolic actions: Bowing, kneeling, saluting, raising our hands, waving, standing at attention, shaking a fist. All of these actions are meant to convey a certain meaning, such as respect, greetings, victory, anger, and so forth.

And how about symbolic colors? "That man has a yellow streak." "He was red with anger." "She has a green thumb." "I'm feeling blue today."

Wow, did you have any idea you lived a life so steeped in symbolism? Where did you learn it all? How did you acquire it? Through osmosis—simply by living in your particular culture.

Of course, different cultures can assign different meanings to the same symbols. For example, in our Western culture, crossing our legs when we sit is merely a way to get comfortable. But in Thailand, if you direct the sole of your foot at someone, it is considered an insult. In England, if you make a V with your fingers pointing up, it means the same things it does in North America: peace. But if you point those same two fingers down, it's the same as giving someone the middle finger.

Scripturally speaking, we cannot escape symbols either. All a pastor has to do on a Sunday morning is talk about the "Lamb of God," and we know he is referring to Jesus. He could also say "Lion of Judah" and, once again, if we have read the Bible, we know this also refers to Christ. What about colors in the Bible? I'll bet you know a few symbolic colors. What about red? You got it: blood. White? Holiness or purity. Purple? Royalty. Or consider the tabernacle. Every detail of the structure was awash in symbolism, from the design of the Ark of the Covenant to the number of candles used in each lamp stand.

As Christians, we can decipher many of these symbols, because they have been drilled into us for years.[1] But even people outside of the church can often catch the meaning of these symbols on an intuitive level. That's the beauty of God's symbolic language. The Lord chose certain symbols because we would know instinctively what they meant even without him having to tell us.

That said; some symbols are more difficult to interpret than others. For example, scholars have been arguing for centuries regarding what the number "666" really stands for. They all agree that it represents the Antichrist, but who or what exactly is the Antichrist? Is he an actual individual who will rise up in the future and hold the entire world under his sway? Was John using that number as a code word to refer to the Roman Emperor at the time? Or does it refer to any leader who rises up against God and his people?

Also, a symbol may have more than one meaning, depending on how it is used. At one point in Scripture, an eagle is used as a symbol of God's judgment (Jeremiah 48:40). Later on, however, it is used as a symbol of how God would intervene to deliver his people from persecution (Revelation 12:14). So we must be wary of leaping to conclusions about what a particular symbol means. This is one way that God's symbolic language keeps drawing us back to him. It is not enough simply to learn the signs and symbols. This isn't a game or a party trick. We must constantly present these signs and symbols to God so he can interpret them for us. Learning to understand God's symbolic language is important, but it is not designed for use outside of relationship with the Creator.

As you can see, symbolism is nothing new. Neither is it a dead form of communication. In fact, with much of the world moving toward images as their main form of communication, symbolic language is more common than ever! That's exciting news, because not only do you have nothing to fear from symbolic language, you are well versed in it already.

Are We Expected to Understand Symbolic Language?

I believe the answer from Scripture is a resounding "Yes!" Remember the story of Elisha scolding Jehoash for striking the ground with the arrows only three times? Consider this example as well:

[The angel] asked me, "What do you see?" I answered, "I see a solid gold lamp stand with a bowl at the top and seven lights on it, with seven channels to the lights Also there are two olive trees by it, one on the right of the bowl the other on the left."

I asked the angel who talked with me, "what are these, my Lord?" He answered, "Do you not know, what these are?"

"No my Lord," I replied.

So he said to me, "This is the word of the Lord to Zerubbabel: 'Not by might nor by power, but by my Spirit,' says the Lord Almighty. (Zechariah 4:2–6)

Why do you think the angel asked Zechariah if he understood what those lamps represented? Why was the angel surprised by Zechariah's response? He assumed that Zechariah—a prophet—would have a working knowledge of the language of the temple and the symbolic ceremonies of his culture.

Read through the Bible and keep track of how many other times the Lord reveals himself and his plans symbolically like this. Is God just trying to be coy? Is he trying to make us look silly because we don't understand? No, he is expressing himself in his native language, a language he expects us all to learn if we are serious about getting to know him.

Here is another interesting story, this time from the New Testament:

Now there was a man of the Pharisees named Nicodemus, a member of the Jewish ruling council.

He came to Jesus at night and said, "Rabbi, we know you are a teacher who has come from God. For no one could perform the miraculous signs you are doing if God were not with him."

"I tell you the truth, unless a man is born again, he cannot see the kingdom of God."

"How can a man be born when he is old?" Nicodemus asked. "Surely he cannot enter a second time into his mother's womb to be born!"

Jesus answered, "I tell you the truth, unless a man is born of water and the Spirit, he cannot enter the kingdom of God.
"How can this be?" Nicodemus asked.
"You are Israel's teacher," said Jesus, "and you do not understand these things?" (John 3:3–5,9–10)

What was Nicodemus missing here? The main theme, of course, was that he did not understand the second birth, the need to be "born again" or "born from above." Jesus scolded Nicodemus for this. But was that really fair? Not even the disciples understood this concept yet. The fact that Jesus was going to die for the sin of the world was still hidden from everyone but Jesus and the Father.

We tend to think Nicodemus didn't get it because he was a Pharisee. He was too caught up in being religious and obeying the law to understand the deep things of God. But something about that assessment reeks of arrogance. In my mind, Nicodemus didn't get it for one very simple reason—the very same reason that makes you and I stumble today: Jesus was speaking symbolically, and Nicodemus was trying to interpret him literally. Nicodemus thought Jesus meant that to be saved, a grown man had to literally climb back into his mother's womb and be born again. No wonder he had a hard time swallowing it. But that wasn't what Jesus was saying at all. He was referring to the baptism of the Holy Spirit, which we witness at the beginning of Acts. To see the Kingdom of God, all men must first be born of water—natural birth—but they must also be born of the Spirit. Just as the angel rebuked Zechariah, "You don't understand these things?" Jesus rebuked Nicodemus, who also should have known these things. As a teacher of the law, Nicodemus knew a good portion of the Old Testament by heart. That included highly symbolic books like Daniel, Ezekiel, and Jeremiah. If anyone in Israel should have been able to think symbolically, it should have been him. And yet, "You are Israel's teacher," said Jesus, "and you don't understand these things?"

The Disciples Go to Symbolic Language School

When the disciples asked Jesus why he spoke to the people in parables, Jesus responded as follows:

> *"The knowledge of the secrets of the kingdom of heaven has been given to you, but not to them.*
>
> *"Whoever has will be given more, and he will have an abundance. Whoever does not have, even what he has will be taken from him.*
>
> *"This is why I speak to them in parables: 'Though seeing, they do not see; though hearing, they do not hear or understand.'*
>
> *"In them is fulfilled the prophecy of Isaiah: 'You will be ever hearing but never understanding; you will be ever seeing but never perceiving.'*
>
> *"For this people's heart has become calloused; they hardly hear with their ears, and they have closed their eyes. Otherwise they might see with their eyes, hear with their ears, understand with their hearts and turn, and I would heal them.*
>
> *"But blessed are your eyes because they see, and your ears because they hear.*
>
> *"For I tell you the truth, many prophets and righteous men longed to see what you see but did not see it, and to hear what you hear but did not hear it." (Matthew 13:11–17)*

I used to think this passage meant that God hid everything in parables (symbolic language) precisely so the people could not understand what he was saying. He always gave the disciples the answers, but he kept everyone else in the dark. Then, I presumed, God was going to judge the people for not being able to hear and understand. Today, I think that such an interpretation is neither true nor logical.

Think about it: Would it be fair if a teacher gave the entire class an algebra test and then slipped an answer sheet to some of his favorite students? Would it then be fair for the teacher to rebuke the rest of the class (those without the answer sheet) for their low scores? Of course not! However, that is exactly what I used to think Jesus was doing with the Jewish nation. The common people just got the test, but the disciples got the test *and* the answer sheet. That is what made them blessed. And I do not think I was alone in my interpretation. The problem is, such an interpretation of this passage does not square with God's character. God is just, and to do such a thing would be the height of injustice.

So what is really going on here? When Jesus told the disciples that they were blessed to be able to see and hear, he was not congratulating them on being fortunate enough to have the answer key. He was congratulating them on having learned to hear and understand God's heavenly, symbolic language, the language people throughout Scripture had to learn if they hoped to understand the deep things of God. By learning to decode Jesus' parables, the disciples were unwittingly enrolled in language school. They were students of the best teacher ever regarding how to hear and interpret the mysteries of God.

God wanted them to understand him. But before they could unearth God's concealed truth, they had to develop the hearts of seekers. It is God's glory to conceal a matter, yes, but he does not force anyone to seek it out. The Jewish nation had been schooled in God's symbolic language in the past, but they had forgotten how to read it, because they had drifted away from God. That is why they had become so hard of hearing. Nevertheless, Jesus was still trying to get them to search out the truth, to help them develop the hearts of true seekers and re-establish relationship with him. Thus, Jesus didn't just give people the answers, but he did tell them where they might be found.

> But Peter said to Him, "Explain this proverb to us."
> And He [Jesus] said, "Are you also even yet dull and igno-rant? Do you not see and understand that whatever goes into the mouth passes into the abdomen and so passes on into the place where discharges are deposited?" (Mark 7:17–19, AMP)

Here is even more proof that Jesus wanted his students to get beyond the point where he had to spoon-feed answers to them. When Peter asked for the answer sheet, Jesus quoted the same section of Isaiah that he used to describe the people of Israel back in Matthew 13! It just goes to show that Jesus was not telling the disciples they were blessed because they got all the answers. They were blessed because he had chosen them as his disciples, because they had the hearts of learners and a hunger for righteousness. Jesus was telling Peter that he had fallen into the deaf ears/blind eyes camp because he could not figure out this parable, this symbolic language on his own. This was a sign that Peter was spiritually dull, that he was not in close relationship with his Creator.

Ongoing Lessons

When they went across the lake, the disciples forgot to take bread. "Be careful," Jesus said to them. "Be on your guard against the yeast of the Pharisees and the Sadducees."

They discussed this among themselves and said, "It is because we didn't bring any bread."

Aware of their discussion, Jesus asked, "You of little faith. Why are you talking among yourselves about having no bread? Do you still not understand? Don't you remember the five loaves for the five thousand, and how many basketfuls you gathered? Or the seven loaves for the four thousand, and how many basketfuls you gathered? How is it you don't understand that I was not talking to you about bread? But be on your guard against the yeast of the Pharisees and Sadducees."

Then they understood that he was not telling them to guard against the yeast in bread, but against the teaching of the Pharisees and the Sadducees. (Matthew 16: 5–12)

Once again, Jesus did not just give his disciples the answer; he let them find it for themselves. When the disciples failed to come up with the right answer though, Jesus became exasperated with them. "How is it you don't understand?" This sounds like a question a parent asks a child after explaining something over and over. Jesus could not believe that, after all his teaching, they were still thinking literally and not interpreting the symbolic meaning behind what he was telling them. He was certain they were farther ahead in the language of the Spirit!

I find the end of this section particularly interesting. Jesus repeats the parable about the yeast of the Pharisees, but he does not interpret it. Even so, the disciples are able to figure it out—not because they were given the answer sheet but because, this time, they pondered what Jesus said until they came up with the answer. Maybe they weren't so dull after all...

The Continuing Story

> *But when he, the Spirit of truth, comes, he will guide you into all truth. He will not speak on his own; he will speak only what he hears, and he will tell you what is yet to come. He will bring glory to me by taking from what is mine and making it known to you. (John 16:13–14)*

In this passage, Jesus was preparing his disciples for his upcoming death. He was comforting them and telling them that they would not be abandoned. Someone—the Holy Spirit—would come in his place and act as their "uplink" to God.

We see the fulfillment of this prophecy in Acts 2 on the day of Pentecost. As the crowd watched in amazement at the outpouring of the Holy Spirit, Peter explained what was happening by quoting the prophet Joel:

> *In the last days, God says, "I will pour out my Spirit on all people. Your sons and daughters will prophecy, your young men will see visions and your old men will dream dreams." (Acts 2:17)*

To put it in plain language, when the Holy Spirit is poured out, God will speak to us in the heavenly language of symbolism. It did not take long for this to begin happening.

Are You Ready?

Now that you know that it is possible to understand God's symbolic language, only one question remains: How motivated are you to learn it? Are you just interested in earning a passing grade? Or do you truly desire to be intimate with God and understand Him in the deepest way possible? Let us all reach for the highest goal. After all, learning the language of the Spirit is not just about gaining information. It is about falling deeper in love with the Creator of that language, our Lord.

[1] For more information about symbols in Scripture, I highly recommend *Interpreting the Symbols and Types* by Kevin Connor. In addition to explaining what biblical symbols mean in various contexts, he also puts these symbols into chronological order so you can see how their usage and interpretation change over time.

Chapter Six

TEN PROPHETIC QUESTIONS

A study was done at an elementary school to determine what effect removing the fence from the perimeter of the schoolyard would have on the students. To the surprise of everyone involved, rather than venture out of the schoolyard or hang out near the perimeter, the students tended to stay close to the middle of the schoolyard. Only when the fence was reinstalled did the children play along the perimeter again. The researchers concluded that although the fence served to restrict the children's movements, it also provided a sense of safety and protection.

Worldviews or paradigms are no different. They offer us a feeling of security. That is why we cling to them so strongly. Our paradigm tells us who we are, where we're going, and where we came from. While our paradigm may appear restrictive, these behavioral boundaries serve a valuable function. Without this "fence," we would be afraid to venture out into the world the same way the children were afraid to venture out of the schoolyard.

With this in mind, how would you respond if the fence around your schoolyard—your paradigm—suddenly disappeared? What if how you saw the world changed completely? What if you were still looking at the same picture as everyone else but saw something completely different? How would you be able to tell if such a radical paradigm shift was from

God? What type of confirmation would you look for? How could you be sure where the new boundary lay?

This is exactly the predicament the Apostle Peter encountered in Acts 10. Even after all the work Jesus had done in his life, Peter still clung to a paradigm that was in need of a drastic change. Peter had no knowledge of his need. In fact, nobody in his culture had any knowledge of his or her need. They thought their paradigm was doing its job just fine. Of all people, the Jews knew where the fences were, and they were sure to stay within the boundaries.

But God, in his great mercy, brought Peter through an experience that changed his paradigm completely. That experience is going to form the focus of the next few chapters. As I walk you through it, I will introduce ten prophetic questions that Peter used to gain an understanding of what God was doing. Here they are in brief:

- If this were a dream, what would it mean?
- Do you see any evidence of colloquialisms or wordplay?
- Is there a connection between the symbolic events and events in your church, community, nation or the world at large?
- Do you see evidence of divine timing?
- Do events correspond with any significant dates, such as holidays, celebrations, or anniversaries?
- Do you notice any significant numbers?
- How do these events correspond to symbolic language in the Bible?
- Is there evidence of a paradigm-shift, particularly from pride to humility, in the people involved?
- Can you organize these events into a prophetic timeline?
- How does God want you to respond?

You will note that I have not numbered these questions, because rarely will you ask these questions in the same order twice, with perhaps the exception of the first and last questions. So, even though we approach them in a particular order in this book, please do not let that restrict how you use them to solve your own prophetic puzzles.

These questions helped Peter understand and interpret the symbolic language God was using to challenge his paradigm. These questions were extremely important to Peter, because they were all he had to go on. As you watch Peter and the New Testament church put this puzzle together, I trust that you will begin to see how these same prophetic questions can also help you assemble the puzzles God gives you today.

Chapter Seven

IF THIS WERE A DREAM, WHAT WOULD IT MEAN?

*A*bout noon the following day as they were approaching the city, Peter went up on the roof to pray. He became hungry and wanted something to eat, and while the meal was being prepared he fell into a trance. He saw heaven open and something like a large sheet being let down to earth by it's four corners. It contained all kinds of four-footed animals as well as reptiles of the earth and the birds of the air. Then a voice told him, "Get up Peter. Kill and eat."

"Surely not, Lord!" Peter replied. "I have never eaten anything impure or unclean."

The voice spoke to him a second time, "Do not call anything impure that God has made clean."

This happened three times, and immediately the sheet was taken back to heaven. (Acts 10:9–16)

Almost immediately following this vision, three men appeared at the door asking Peter to come with them to see a Gentile named Cornelius. Because of this vision and Peter's obedience, the entire Gentile world was brought into the kingdom of heaven.

If you were God, would you entrust such a pivotal event to mere symbols, which could easily be misinterpreted? You would if symbolism were your native language. You would if it were the job of the Holy Spirit to speak in the language Jesus used with the disciples while on earth. And you would if the person you were speaking to had been adequately schooled in that language.

Walls Within Walls

One of the most important boundaries in Peter's worldview was to refrain from social contact with Gentiles. A favorite prayer of the Pharisees was "Thank you Lord that you did not make me a Gentile, a woman or a dog." A Jew could converse with a Gentile concerning business, but that was it. To eat with a Gentile was to be ostracized from your community or possibly even be killed. To eat non-kosher foods—foods not permitted by Jewish law—could lead to the same consequences. Society would boot you over the collective fence, never to be allowed back in!

If a Jew during Peter's time could give his fence or worldview a name, it would be this: "set apart." To be set apart meant obeying all sorts of religious customs and rituals, such as ceremonial hand washing, feasts, sacrifices, and prayers. All of these practices reached their zenith in the temple. To a Jew, the temple was the culmination of everything it meant to be Jewish. It was there that children were brought to be dedicated and sacrifices made. It was there that Yahweh was said to dwell. Seeing as the temple was such a large part of what it meant to be Jewish, let's look at how the temple was set up and how this structure affected the Jewish worldview:

The temple consisted of a number of segregated courts, listed here in order from outermost to innermost:

1) The court of the Gentiles
2) The court of the women
3) The court of the Jewish men (ages 12 and up)
4) The court of the priests
5) The court of the holies

6) The Holy of Holies (This was where the Ark of the Covenant rested, behind a curtain that was 24 inches wide and 25 feet high. Once a year, the High Priest entered the Holy of Holies to offer sacrifices on behalf of the nation.)

As you can see, Peter's faith taught him that there were many barriers through which one had to pass before reaching God. As a Jewish man, Peter was two steps closer to God than a Gentile. Even if a Gentile converted to Judaism, the outer court was as far as he was allowed to go. Peter could see that the temple separated Jews from Gentiles, men from women, and the priests from other Jewish men. However, the person that the temple kept separate from virtually everyone was God. It is no wonder that Peter and his fellow Jews had developed a worldview that told them they were separate from—even better than—the Gentiles.

This was no longer true for Peter and his fellow Jewish Christians, however. Remember, when Christ died, the curtain was ripped in two. Now everyone, not just the high priest, could access God by faith. But what about circumcision? What about the feasts? The sacrifices? The ceremonial hand washing? As far as Peter knew, even after Christ's death and resurrection, these rules were still in effect. Why should they change? Even Christ had followed them when he was on earth. Peter's paradigm had included these practices since the day he was born. He had never eaten anything outside of the law. He wouldn't dream of it! That would be turning his back on centuries of tradition. Peter's fence line was intact. He knew his boundaries, and he lived happily within them, as did everyone he knew. Little did Peter realize his entire fence was about to come crashing down.

After Christ's death and resurrection, the temple was still the center of the Christian belief system and worldview. You could be a good Jew and a good Christian at the same time. At this point, the early believers thought only Jews could be Christians, so the temple was now about Jesus, the Jewish Savior. That was about to change though. Through Peter, God would pluck the Gentiles from the outer court and plant them right in the middle of the Holy of Holies. They wouldn't even need to wash their hands (or get circumcised for that matter). It was time to move the fence line.

Peter's Journey on God's Timeline Begins

Knowing all this, I wouldn't be surprised if the first thing Peter thought after seeing the vision recorded in Acts 10:9–16 was "Get behind me, Satan!" This vision challenged everything Peter held to be true. And if it were true, then it would cost Peter everything he had.

To determine whether or not this vision was from God, Peter had to take the vision apart and look for clues of God's involvement, his divine fingerprints. It was only natural for Peter to ask the first of our prophetic questions while he waited for his supper:

If this were a dream, what would it mean?

Peter began where every prophet began, by *pondering*. Instead of interpreting the vision on a literal level, as in, "God must want me to kill and eat some unclean animals," Peter tried to figure out what the animals symbolized. Pondering is a gift from God. It is his way of getting our attention, slowing us down, and pulling us into his divine perspective. Riddles like this are designed to make us ponder. They also serve to test our hearts. How serious are we about hearing God and doing what he says? If we encounter something that makes us do a double take, will we allow ourselves to be pulled into his divine perspective? Or will we merely pass it off as a result of the pizza we ate last night? As Brad Jersak says in his book *Can You Hear Me? Tuning In to the God Who Speaks,* we tend to ask ourselves, "Was that God or just my imagination?" And then we quickly assume it was the latter.

I do not think many of us would have pondered Peter's vision for very long. Bound as we are to reason, we would have dismissed it as merely a symptom of our hunger. We would have looked for an excuse to pass it off, to hold on to our current paradigm. Perhaps, feeling faint, we had dozed off and had a brief dream. Unfortunately, it is exactly this sort of thinking that so often aborts the divine communication process.

Not realizing that symbolic language is designed to lead us into a deeper understanding of reality, we stay within the perceived safety of our current belief system, and then we wonder why we can't hear God.

If Peter had taken this same approach to his vision, where would we be today? Still stuck in the outer courts, probably. Thankfully, as a Jew, Peter knew God takes the things we experience during the day and uses them to teach us in our dreams at night. This is exactly how Jesus taught. He took daily experiences and infused them with spiritual meaning. Peter probably assumed that God was doing the same thing with his vision. He knew the point of symbolic language was to enable him to see something different than his current belief system allowed him to see, and Peter was curious to find out what that "something" was.

Chapter Eight

DIVINE WORDPLAY

To ponder his vision properly and uncover the puzzle pieces hidden within, Peter would have had to ask a second prophetic question:

Is there any evidence of divine wordplay?

Colloquialisms, idioms, rhymes, puns—God tends to use them virtually every time he communicates with his people. Here is an excellent example from Jeremiah, with which Peter would probably have been well acquainted:

> *The word of the Lord came to me, "What do you see, Jeremiah?"*
> *"I see the branch of an almond tree," I replied.*
> *The Lord said, "You have seen correctly, for I am watching to see that my word is fulfilled." (Jeremiah 1:11–13)*

Why would God give Jeremiah a picture of an almond branch and say it had something to do with watching for his word to be fulfilled? In Hebrew, the word for "hasten" (*shoked ani*), which is translated as "watching" in the NIV, is very similar to the word for "almond tree" (*shoked*). The almond tree was named "hasten" because it produced flowers, leaves, and fruit early. Thus, it "hastened" to produce. This mirrored what the Lord was saying about his word. He was going to "hasten" his word to produce. The Great Author was using local symbols and idioms from Jeremiah's culture to get his message across.

Summer Fruit

Another example of divine wordplay that may have come to Peter's mind is a conversation between God and the prophet Amos:

> *Thus the Lord showed me: Behold, a basket of summer fruit.*
> *And he said to me, "Amos, what do you see?" So I said, "A basket of summer fruit."*
> *Then the Lord said to me: "The end has come upon my people Israel; I will not pass by them anymore." (Amos 8:1–2)*

Why would the Lord show Amos something that appears to have no connection with their conversation? To answer that question, you need to know something about the Jewish concept of summer fruit. Summer fruit was the last fruit to be harvested each year. It was usually withered when it came off the vine and began to rot quickly. Beginning to see the connection? Just as summer fruit was almost at the point of being rotten, so was Israel. This comparison was not lost on Amos. He saw the nation's rot, even though Israel still saw itself as fresh fruit. God was telling Amos that Israel's season of fruitfulness was at an end. Pruning time had come.

Zephaniah

Zephaniah 2:4 would also have been familiar to Peter: "Gaza will be abandoned and Ashkelon left in ruins. At midday Ashdod will be emptied and Ekron uprooted." Why did these particular cities receive judgments against them in this particular order? Once again, if we go back to the Hebrew, we find a play on words.

In Hebrew, "Gaza" (which means "strong") is *azzah*. "Abandoned," in Hebrew is *azab*. So if we substitute in the Hebrew words, this sentence says, "*Azzah* will be *azab*." Furthermore, "Ekron," or *Eqrown* means "eradication" in Hebrew. And "uprooted" is *aqar*. So the second part of this verse becomes "*Eqrown* will be *aqar*." If you look in a concordance, you will also note that "Ekron" is actually derived from the word *aqar*, so the meaning of the two words is extremely close. To put this in modern terms, this would be like saying, "Equador will be acquitted, Spain will be slain, and France has no chance." It just goes to show that God is more playful than we give him credit for.

Who's Afraid of the Big, Bad Barley?

In obedience to God's command, Gideon had assembled his army to fight the Midianites, but they were still a little spooked. So the Lord told Gideon to sneak down to the Midianite camp and listen to what the enemy was saying. God said that Gideon would be encouraged by what he heard.

> Gideon arrived just as a man was telling a friend a dream.
> "I had a dream," he was saying. "A round loaf of barley bread came tumbling into the Midianite camp. It struck the tent with such force that the tent overturned and collapsed."
> His friend responded, "This can be nothing other than the sword of Gideon the son of Joash the Israelite. God has given the Midianites and the whole camp into his hands."
> When Gideon heard the dream and its interpretation, he worshipped God. (Judges 7:13–15)

Why a barley cake? When it came to flour, barley was always second choice. It was the food of the poor—of the people the Midianites had oppressed. With the Midianites stealing all the choice wheat, barley was all the people had left. Thus, when the Midianites talked of Gideon, they referred to him as barley, not fine wheat like them. God used this colloquial expression to his advantage in the dream. That is why the Midianites had such an easy time interpreting the dream. They realized immediately that they were about to be rolled over by someone they saw as inferior—Gideon.[1]

Peter's Name

Jesus followed in the tradition of the Old Testament by using wordplay in his teachings and discussions. One of the best examples I can think of occurs in Matthew 16:13–18.

> *When Jesus came into the region of Caesarea Philippi, He asked his disciples, saying, "Who do men say that I, the Son of Man, am?"*
>
> *So they said, "Some say John the Baptist, some Elijah, and others, Jeremiah or one of the prophets."*
>
> *He said to them, "But who do you say that I am?"*
>
> *Simon Peter answered and said, "You are the Christ, the Son of the living God."*
>
> *Jesus answered and said to him, "Blessed are you, Simon Bar-Jonah, for flesh and blood has not revealed this to you, but My Father who is in heaven.*
>
> *"And I say to you that you are Peter [Petros], and on this rock [petra] I will build my church, and the gates of Hades will not prevail against it."*

This is probably one of the most disputed passages in Scripture. While both Catholics and Protestants recognize that Jesus was using a play on words to make a point, they disagree on exactly what that point is.

Petros means "stone," and *petra* (the feminine version of *petros*) means "rock ledge or cliff." Why would Jesus call Peter a feminine version of his own name? Simple. Jesus wasn't using the word *petra* in reference to Peter; he was referring to Peter's *testimony*. In other words, Jesus would build his Church on the basis of Peter's testimony—that Jesus was the Messiah—not on Peter himself.

The Branch

One final example, also from Christ's ministry: "And he came and dwelt in a city called Nazareth that it might be fulfilled, which was *spoken by the prophets*, "He shall be called a Nazarene" (Matthew 2:23).

114

This quote references the fact that Joseph took Mary and Jesus to live in Nazareth after returning from Egypt. Matthew is arguing here that this move fulfilled a prophecy from the Old Testament that stated Jesus would be called a Nazarene. There is only one problem with this interpretation: Nowhere in the Old Testament does it state that the Messiah would live in a town called Nazareth. In fact, the word "Nazareth" does not even appear in the Old Testament. So what is Matthew talking about? Here's a hint: "A shoot will come up from the stump of Jesse; from his roots a Branch shall bear fruit" (Isaiah 11:1).

In Hebrew, the word for "branch" is "*nester.*" The word "Nazareth" is based on the word *nester.* So a Nazarene would be known as a "branch." That means, as Matthew says, Joseph's move to Nazareth meant that the prophecy in Isaiah would be fulfilled. By becoming a resident of Nazareth, Jesus became a *nester* or "branch."

Back to Peter and the Sheet

With his knowledge of how God used wordplay, idioms, and colloquialisms, Peter would have paid attention to this device as he pondered this vision. If so, what would he have found? Let's look at his description of how the sheet was taken up into heaven:

> But Peter said, "Not so, Lord! For I have never eaten anything common or unclean."
> And the voice spoke to him again the second time, "What God has cleansed you must not call common."
> This was done three times. And the object was taken up into heaven again. (Acts 10:14–16)

The word *analambanol,* which Peter used in the vision for "taken up," is the same term Luke used to describe how Jesus was taken up into heaven: "Until the day he [Jesus] was *taken up* to heaven, after giving instructions through the Holy Spirit to the apostles he had chosen" (Acts 1:2). *Analambanol* means, "to take up, receive up." It implies God supernaturally drawing something up unto himself.

Recently, Peter had seen Jesus taken up into heaven, a scene he would never forget. Once again in his vision, Peter saw something ascend into heaven. God was reaching down and laying hold of something by his supernatural power. This time it was a sheet full of unclean animals. We know that Peter caught the meaning of this visual pun, because he used the same term to describe it as Luke used to describe Jesus' ascension. To Peter, this was a sign of God's involvement. It probably helped to convince him that his vision was not totally blasphemous. Now Peter was free to ask a number of other prophetic questions that would help him further decode the baffling picture.

[1] Jim Goll. "Handling Dreams, Visions, and Revelations." Study Notes. *Ministry to the Nations*, p. 28.

Chapter Nine

SIGNIFICANT
NUMBERS

Peter had been drawn into pondering this vision and had completed his scan for figures of speech. Now he proceeded to the next prophetic question:

Do you notice any significant numbers?

The Jews did not just use numbers for mathematics or to find a friend's street address. They were a crucial part of God's symbolic language. In fact, one of the angels named in Daniel 8:13 is Palmoni, which means "numberer of secrets."

You probably know some significant biblical numbers already. For example, what does the number "666" mean to you? Even if you've never read the Bible, you probably know that "666" stands for the Antichrist. That's because, according to the biblical writers, "6" is the number of Man (because he was created on the sixth day). It is one number short of God's number "7," which signifies perfection. The Jews often multiplied or repeated things for emphasis. So the *Anti*christ's number became "666," meaning "the worst."

How about the number "40"? How many times does this number show up in the Bible?

- 40 days and nights of rain during the Flood (Genesis 7:4).
- Moses hiding out in Midian for 40 years after he killed the Egyptian (Genesis 15:13).
- The Israelites wandering in the desert for 40 years before entering the Promised Land (Exodus 16:35).
- Jesus tempted by the devil after fasting in the wilderness for 40 days (Matthew 4:1–11).

In all of these cases (and there are many more), what does the number "40" represent? Usually, testing or purification. The 40 days or years were like a waiting period during which people were made ready to move on to the next step.

Then there's the number "12." This number usually symbolizes divine government or authority.

- 12 rulers (Genesis 17:20)
- 12 tribes (Genesis 42:13/Joshua 4:2)
- 12 disciples (Matthew 10:2)
- 12 gates into the New Jerusalem (Revelation 21:10–12) and twelve foundations (Revelation 21:14)
- 12 fruits on the tree of life (Revelation 22:2)

Knowing this, could Peter find still more of God's fingerprints in his vision through the use of divine numbers? Let's take a look:

> But Peter said, "Not so, Lord! For I have never eaten anything common or unclean."
>
> And the voice spoke to him again the second time, "What God has cleansed you must not call common."
>
> This was done three times. And the object was taken up into heaven again. (Acts 10:14–16)

Peter made sure to point out that the vision of the sheet, his denial, and God's rebuke were all repeated three times. Peter also emphasized this numerical fact to the council in Jerusalem when explaining why he believed his vision was from God (Acts 11:10). Why would the number of times this sequence is repeated be significant to Peter and the council? Did this somehow authenticate his vision as divine?

Peter's Love/Hate Relationship With the Number Three

In Scripture, the number three is a mark of the divine (Father, Son, and Holy Spirit) and of confirmation (cf. Deuteronomy 19:15; Matthew 18: 16, 20; 1 Corinthians 14:29). Peter would have been aware of this. But he had his own unique relationship with the number three as well.

Peter and the Rooster

Peter answered and said to Him [Jesus], "Even if all are made to stumble because of you, I will never be made to stumble."
Jesus said to him, "Assuredly I say to you, that this night, before the rooster crows, you will deny me three times." (Matthew 26:33–34)

This prophecy came true with chilling accuracy for Peter. When the rooster crowed immediately following Peter's third denial of Jesus, Jesus looked straight at him, and Peter suddenly realized that, once again, he was suffering from a bout of "foot in mouth disease."

In Matthew 27–28, we read of Jesus' death and resurrection. The sky grew dark for *three* hours as Jesus hung on the middle cross between two thieves. *Three* crosses. And on the *third* day, he rose from the dead. While these events did not involve Peter directly, I am certain they would have been fresh in his mind as he saw the sheet descend from heaven three times.

After realizing his utter and complete failure to remain loyal to Jesus, Peter went back to the only other thing he knew: fishing. Peter was in quite a state after all that had happened. He had denied Jesus. He was off the team. But Jesus had a different plan for Peter, one that did not involve him coming home reeking of fish every day. Jesus was about to call Peter out of his premature retirement.

*He [Jesus] said to him [Peter] the third time, "Simon, son of
Jonah, do you love me?"*

*Peter was grieved because he had said to him the third time,
"do you love me?"*

*And he said to Him, "Lord, You know all things; you
know that I love you." Jesus said to him, "Feed my sheep."*
(John 21:17)

Once again, Jesus questioned Peter regarding what came out of his
mouth. But, just as Peter had denied Jesus three times, now Jesus reinstated him three times. When he was certain of Peter's commitment,
he allowed Peter to re-join the team.

*And behold Moses and Elijah appeared to Him [Jesus], talking
with him. Then Peter answered and said to Jesus, "Lord, it is
good for us to be here; if you wish, let us make three tabernacles:
one for you, one for Moses, and one for Elijah."*

*While he was still speaking, behold, a bright cloud overshad-
owed them: and suddenly a voice came out of the cloud, saying,
"This is my beloved Son, in whom I am well pleased. Hear Him!"*
(Matthew 17:3–5)

Here we have two sets of three: 1) Jesus, Moses, and Elijah and 2) Peter,
James, and John. Peter was so excited at what was going on that he began
talking without thinking, inserting his foot directly into his mouth once
again. As he began to jabber about building shelters for Moses, Elijah,
and Jesus, God humbled him.

A Familiar Pattern

At first, this vision may have felt like a return to Peter's past foibles. The
pattern of events was the same: 1) Peter made a strong statement, 2) he
was rebuked, 3) and the scene repeated itself three times. I'm sure Peter
was thinking, "I've been down this road before. This time I'm going to

get it right. I'm going to think before I speak and see where this is all going to lead. If this is the Lord, something good will come out of it, and I will see it soon!"

Sure enough, God was playing off Peter's past experience as well as his knowledge of Scripture to reinforce the fact that he was the source of Peter's vision. This is another great example of how God speaks to us within the context of our experience.

Despite the fact that the numbers added up, a huge question remained: How could this vision be from God when it went against everything Peter held dear: his culture, his family, his education, his religious upbringing, even his national identity? To discover the answer to this riddle, Peter had to ask still more prophetic questions.

Chapter Ten

BACK TO THE BIBLE

As I have already noted, one of Peter's first responses to his vision would have been to interpret the various elements in light of Scripture. This is no less important for us to do today. The book of Proverbs says as much, noting that in addition to providing us with wisdom and discipline, the proverbs are also useful for understanding words of insight and understanding parables, sayings, and riddles of the wise (Proverbs 1:1–6). So get a good concordance, a Bible dictionary, and some commentaries. Use these tools to help you understand what things meant to the biblical writers when they actually wrote them, not just what you think they mean today. I also highly recommend Kevin Conner's *Interpreting the Symbols and Types*. In this book, Kevin goes through the entire Bible and shows you the patterns of numbers, colors, actions, objects, and animals and explains how the meaning of these symbols changed over time.

Two Other Sources of Interpretation

Even though we should always start with the Bible, we don't need to stop there. When seeking to interpret a dream, a vision or actual events, we need to remember that symbolism can emerge from two other main sources as well:

1) *Culture:* If God is addressing an entire nation; he often appropriates symbols that have significance for that nation. You will see a number of examples of this when we get to the case studies in

this book. However, for now, a good example is how God used the destruction of the temple to speak to the Jews during the time of Ezekiel. The Jews regarded the temple as the sign of God's presence and blessing amongst them, to the point where they thought they could live any way they wanted, just as long as the temple remained. To teach the Jews that obedience was more important than religious rituals, God allowed the temple to be destroyed by the Babylonians and the Jews to be carried off into exile. This was a powerful, real life object lesson that they would never forget.

2) *Personal experiences:* These are some of the trickiest symbols to interpret, because their meanings are so particular. For example, what does a dog mean to you? I have two friends, both of whom are pastors, and when they dream of dogs, it means two completely different things. To one of them, it means the Lord is coming to help and to save. To the other, it means the enemy is coming to attack. How is this possible? When they were children, they had two very different experiences with dogs: One was saved by a dog, and the other was attacked by a dog. This is a good example of how the same symbol can mean different things to different people. So don't be too hasty to help someone decode such symbols until you know more about their own personal attachment to them.

Breaking Things Down

Knowing all of this, Peter would have begun analyzing the following details of his vision in light of the Bible: 1) heaven opening, 2) the way the sheet descended and was taken back up into heaven, 3) the voice, 4) the sheet itself, and 5) the animals. Let's see how he might have interpreted them.

Heaven Opening

Most assuredly, I say to you, hereafter you shall see heaven open, and the angels of God ascending and descending on the Son of Man. (John 1:51)

In the above verse, Jesus described the way heaven opened for Jacob, Elijah, and other patriarchs and prophets in the Scriptures.

Then [Joseph] dreamed, and behold, a ladder was set upon the earth, and its top reached to heaven, and there the angels of God were ascending and descending on it. (Genesis 28:12)

Then it happened as they continued on and talked, that suddenly a chariot of fire appeared with horses of fire, and separated the two of them, and Elijah went up by a whirlwind into heaven. (2Kings 2:11)

In both of these cases, heaven opened, and they could see what was going on "upstairs." A few times, people were even asked to go to a high place before the Lord would open heaven (cf. Exodus 24 and Matthew 17:1–7). Heaven was located "above," at least symbolically, and Scripture stated as much. Besides heaven being above, when it opened, people, angels, and even Jesus himself ascended to it.

I am sure Peter had these passages in mind when he contemplated his vision. Even though Peter's vision may not have seemed in the least bit biblical at first, it did fit how the scriptures said things worked.

The Animals

Leviticus 11 makes a clear division between animals that are ceremonially "clean" and those that are "unclean." Examples of clean animals include cows, fish, and grasshoppers. Unclean animals included fish without scales, pigs, and owls. The Jews were free to eat the clean animals, but they weren't even to go near the carcasses of the unclean animals. Many scholars have debated why God made these distinctions. Some say he did it to keep his people separated from the idolatry associated with these unclean animals in surrounding nations. Others argue that God made this distinction for health reasons, that the animals labeled as unclean often carried diseases or had some other quality that made them unfit for human consumption. At any rate, when Peter saw the animals, his mind would have flown immediately to this aspect of Jewish law. But why did the vision mix the unclean animals with the clean ones? Was God going back on his word?

The Voice

And a voice came to him, "Rise, Peter; kill and eat."
(Acts 10:13)

At this point in his life, Peter was probably accustomed to hearing voices from heaven, such as during the transfiguration:

> *While he was still speaking, behold, a bright cloud overshadowed them, and suddenly a voice came out of the cloud saying, "This is my beloved Son, in whom I am well pleased. Hear Him! (Matthew 17:5)*

Peter also would have read about similar heavenly pronouncements in Scripture, incidents where God allowed his voice to be heard but did not reveal himself.

> *The words were still on his lips when a voice came from heaven, "This is what is decreed for you, King Nebuchadnezzar: Your royal authority has been taken from you. (Daniel 4:31)*
> *And I heard the voice of the Lord saying, "Whom shall I send, and who will go for us?" (Isaiah 6:8)*
> *Suddenly a voice came to him, "What are you doing here Elijah?" (1 Kings 19:13)*

Even though the pattern of God speaking from heaven was familiar, we have already seen that what the voice was telling Peter to do wasn't exactly kosher. It was asking him to kill and eat animals that were forbidden for a Jew to even touch. Could the Scriptures help Peter figure out this strange command as well? Just imagine if, like Peter, you had heard the following verse all of your life:

> *Nevertheless, you may slaughter your animals in any of your towns and eat as much of the meat as you want, as if it were gazelle or deer, according to the blessing the LORD your God gives you. Both the ceremonially unclean and the clean may eat it. (Deuteronomy 12:15)*

Do you think you would have noticed a connection? I find it particularly interesting that God said both the ceremonially unclean and the clean could eat the meat. Just as in Peter's vision, we see a mingling of things that traditionally were not allowed to go together. Would Peter have noticed this as well?

The Sheet

How about the sheet in which the animals descended? Could the sheet also be a coded message from the Scriptures? Before you answer, take a look at this passage from Isaiah:

> *On this mountain the LORD Almighty will prepare a feast of rich food for all peoples, a banquet of aged wine—the best of meats and the finest of wines.*
>
> *On this mountain he will destroy the shroud that enfolds all peoples, the sheet that covers all nations; he will swallow up death forever. The Sovereign LORD will wipe away the tears from all faces; he will remove the disgrace of his people from all the earth. The LORD has spoken. In that day they will say, 'Surely this is our God; we trusted in him, and he saved us. This*

is the LORD, we trusted in him; let us rejoice and be glad in his salvation.' (Isaiah 25:6–9)

This passage uses an image of a sheet or a shroud to describe the curse of death that covers all nations. It prophesies that at some point, God will destroy that curse, bringing salvation to all. Could God have used this image to make the same point to Peter, that salvation wasn't just for "clean" people but for "unclean" people as well?

Acts 10:11 also indicates that the sheet was tied at the corners. What could this mean? If you are familiar with the Old Testament, as Peter was, you will know that the number "4" in Scripture is often used in association with the earth and nature (cf. Genesis 2:10; Leviticus 11: 20–27; Isaiah 11:12; and Ezekiel 37:9). The book of Revelation also picks up on this usage. *After this I saw four angels standing at the four corners of the earth, holding back the four winds of the earth… (Revelation 7:1)* Therefore, it would not be preposterous to suggest that Peter might have interpreted this word picture to mean that this scriptural promise was finally coming true. God was about to extend his salvation to the four corners of the earth, thus lifting the curse of death from everyone, Jews and Gentiles alike. Was Peter getting warmer? Read on!

Chapter Eleven

DIVINE TIMING

Timing links two events together so that it becomes obvious that such a coincidence could not have happened by chance. Two things must fit together so precisely and in such a remarkable way that they complete each other. To a Jew, such an event was yet another one of God's fingerprints.

"Right Then…"

In Scripture, we should start looking for one of these divinely orchestrated coincidences when we see the words "right then." For example,

> *This happened three times, and then it was all pulled up to heaven again. Right then three men who had been sent to me from Caesarea stopped at the house where I was staying. The Spirit told me to have no hesitation about going with them." (Acts 11:10–11)*

We also see this phrase at the moment of Christ's death:

> *And when Jesus had cried out again in a loud voice, he gave up his spirit.*
>
> *At that moment [Right then!] the curtain of the temple was torn in two from top to bottom. The earth shook and the rocks split.*

The tombs broke open and the bodies of many holy people who had died were raised to life.

They came out of the tombs, and after Jesus' resurrection they went into the holy city and appeared to many people.

When the centurion and those who were guarding Jesus saw the earthquake and all that had happened, they were terrified, and exclaimed, "Surely he was the Son of God!" (Matthew 27:50–54)

How did the centurion and those guarding the cross conclude that Jesus was the Son of God? They put two and two together. The moment Jesus died, all of these other things began to happen. They saw the symbolism behind each of these events, and they believed.

Here is another excellent example of timing as a sign. It concerns a royal official from Capernaum whose son was sick. When he heard Jesus had arrived in Galilee, he went out and begged Jesus to heal his son.

The royal official said, "Sir, come down before my child dies."

Jesus replied, "You may go. Your son will live."

The man took Jesus at his word and departed.

While he was still on his way, his servants met him with the news that his boy was living.

When he inquired as to the time when his son got better, they said to him, "The fever left him yesterday at the seventh hour."

Then the father realized that this was the exact time at which Jesus had said to him, "Your son will live." So he and all his household believed. (John 5:49–53)

Because the timing of his son's recovery matched the timing of Jesus' words, the royal official took it as a sign from God, and believed.

How about timing as a sign in the Old Testament? Here is a good one: Abraham did not want just any wife for his son Isaac. She had to be from his family's clan. So Abraham sent one of his servants back to his homeland and made him vow to bring back a wife for Isaac. Upon arriving at the village, the servant wondered, "How am I going to know which woman is the right one?" He came up with an idea and bounced it off God: "The women from the village are on their way to fetch water from this well. How about if the girl I ask for water offers to serve not only me but my camels as well? Then I will know she is the one for my master's son."

Here is what happened: "Before he had finished praying [right then], Rebekah came out with her jar on her shoulder. She was the daughter of Bethuel son of Milcah, who was the wife of Abraham's brother Nahor" (Genesis 24:15). Just as the servant had requested, she offered to draw water for him as well as his camels. Once again, we see that timing was crucial to confirming that it was God who had spoken. No one but God could have made exactly the right person show up "right then!" When the servant told his story to Rebekah's family, they recognized God's fingerprints on this event immediately. "This is from the Lord; we can say nothing to you one way or the other," said Rebekah's mother and brother. "Take her and go" (Genesis 24:50–51). We will discuss timing in more detail during the case studies in this book. For now, here are some more biblical examples of divine timing for you to research: Exodus 8: 9–11; 1 Samuel 2:34; Ezekiel 33:21–22; Daniel 5:30–31; Luke 1:41, 64; Luke 2:38; and Luke 3:21.

Peter Takes the Plunge

> *While Peter was still thinking about the vision, the Spirit said to him, "Simon, three men are looking for you. So get up and go downstairs. Do not hesitate to go with them, for I have sent them." (Acts 10:19–20)*

When the three men showed up immediately following Peter's vision, Peter probably didn't need the Holy Spirit's urging to convince him that somehow these men and his vision were connected. But Peter might have been a bit more hesitant to heed the Spirit's command had he known a little more about who these men were and why they were looking for him...

Chapter Twelve

MAKING CONNECTIONS

Remember what I said earlier about how God speaks to us in the context of our current experience? That is what our next prophetic question addresses:

Is there a connection between the symbolic event(s) and current events in your life, your church, your community, your nation or the world at large?

Peter knew his vision must have something to do with what his religion and culture taught him was unclean, but what exactly? Apart from the timing of the visitors' arrival, probably one of the first things that struck Peter was how many men were seeking him: *three,* the most significant number of his life. But what did they have to do with the sheet? And why would the Spirit tell Peter to go with these three men and not doubt it was God who was behind it all? Was God trying to prepare Peter for something that *would* cause him to doubt? I wonder if, when Peter heard the Holy Spirit say, "Doubt nothing," he said, "Oh no. Now what?"

Indeed, there was one fact in this whole affair about which the Holy Spirit had yet to inform Peter: The three men at his door were not Jews. They were Gentiles. Pagans.

> *Peter went down and said to the men, "I'm the one you're looking for. Why have you come?"*

The men replied, "We have come from Cornelius the centurion. He is a righteous and God-fearing man, who is respected by all the Jewish people. A holy angel told him to have you come to his house so that he could hear what you have to say."

Then Peter invited the men into the house to be his guests. The next day Peter started out with them, and some of the brothers from Joppa went along. (Acts 10:21–23)

Every aspect of Peter's religious and cultural upbringing told him that he could not associate with these people, never mind travel with them or invite them into his home. To hang out with Gentiles was to take his life into his hands. At this moment, even the Apostle Paul (who was still going by his old name "Saul" at the time) would kill Peter for this act if he could get his hands on him! By inviting them in, Peter broke a major taboo, and eventually, everyone found out about it (Acts 11:2–4). But remember what we said about "right then" moments? Peter's vision was about unclean animals. It was given to him three times. Then, almost immediately afterwards, three "unclean" men appeared at his door. Could this be a coincidence? Not a chance when God is involved.

What was going on in Peter's life at this time into which God might be trying to speak with this vision? Was the question of whether or not the Gentiles could be saved hot on his mind? It doesn't appear that way. Gentiles were unclean. They were the last people on earth Peter expected God to care about. After all, he was right on the scene when Jesus refused to help the Canaanite woman, telling her, "It is not right to take the children's bread and toss it to their dogs" (Matthew 15:22–28). Sure, Jesus helped her in the end, but he didn't seem too happy about it.

So how did Peter's vision fit his context? For one thing, he was hungry. So God spoke to him using food. It was the wrong kind of food—unclean birds, reptiles, and other animals—but food all the same. But that was just Peter's personal, immediate context. What other things were going on in Israel at large that might tie in to what God was telling Peter?

Think back to the crucifixion. Upon witnessing Christ's death, who were some of the first people to declare their faith in Jesus? That's right, *Gentiles,* namely, the Roman centurion and the rest of the men who had been guarding Jesus. Recall also the tearing of the veil in the temple. The path to the Holy of Holies—to God himself—had been cleared by Christ's death. There was no longer any division between Jew and Gentile, man and woman, slave and free. All had equal access to salvation under Christ (Romans 10:12–13).

This change was foreshadowed several times during Christ's ministry:

- Jesus healed the demon-possessed daughter of a Canaanite woman (Matthew 15:22–28).
- Jesus used a Samaritan as an example of a righteous person during one of his parables (Luke 10:30–42).
- Jesus marveled at the faith of the Roman centurion (Matthew 8:5–10).
- Jesus also offered salvation to a Samaritan woman he met while waiting by a well (John 4:1–43). Not only did she come to believe he was the Christ, several of her neighbors did as well. In fact, during this incident, Jesus spoke openly about what was to happen, saying, "Believe me, woman, a time is coming when you will worship the Father neither on this mountain nor in Jerusalem. You Samaritans worship what you do not know; we worship what we do know, for salvation is from the Jews. Yet a time is coming and has now come when the true worshipers will worship the Father in spirit and truth, for they are the kind of worshipers the Father seeks. God is spirit, and his worshipers must worship in spirit and in truth" (John 4:21–24).

So, whether Peter recalled any of these incidents or not when he received his vision, there is no way he could say that God was speaking into a vacuum concerning the Gentiles. He had been softening up the ground for some time now. With Peter's vision, he was about to bring this prophecy to fruition.

Who Let In the Rabbits?

To help you get a better sense of how to make connections between symbols and things going on in your present context, I would like to share a dream God gave me concerning Y2K and my life around that time.

At the time I had this dream, Y2K was gaining a lot of publicity, mostly negative, and there was definitely the possibility of going overboard in preparation. One night I went to bed thinking about this.

That night I dreamt I was walking through my downstairs TV room when I realized the cold storage room door on my left was partly open. Through the crack in the door, I could see something moving around inside.

As I peered through the doorway, I was amazed to see two big, white, fluffy rabbits! I wasn't happy about this at all. Rabbits shouldn't be in the house! I continued upstairs thinking about this when I encountered another rabbit sitting on the stairs. Now I was getting angry! Who let all these rabbits into the house?

When I got upstairs, I noticed my back door was open. Standing in the doorway was a lady I knew. She had a look on her face that told me she knew something I didn't, and she was wondering how long it would take me to figure it out. I told her I didn't want her rabbits in my house. She just smiled and gave me a look that said I would clue in sooner or later.

When I woke up, I wrote the dream out immediately and sat down to ponder what it might mean. I knew it had to do with the Y2K bug, because that was what I went to bed talking to the Lord about. But what did the rabbits signify? What were they doing in my house? I pondered it off and on throughout the week but did not arrive at a clear answer. Then one morning, as I was still thinking about the dream, I went to the washroom to freshen up. As I was washing my face thinking about what a rabbit could possibly symbolize, I happened to look up at a doily hanging on our wall. It was one of those things that had been up for so long I didn't even see it any more. The doily pictured a white rabbit with a little, pink ribbon around its neck. Stitched under the picture in baby blue lettering were the words, "'Home sweet home." Then it hit

136

me: What does a rabbit represent? Rabbits are cute and cuddly, like cats without the claws. They're harmless. That was it! Just as the rabbits were harmless so was Y2K. That was the beginning of my answer!

I also realized that the rabbits were fat, well fed, and had thick winter coats. They had absolutely no reason to worry about the winter. It also occurred to me that breeders always keep male and female rabbits apart, because they multiply so fast. As the saying goes, "They breed like rabbits!"

I noted the significance of the number of rabbits as well. The number three usually represents the Godhead, a number of divine completeness (more on this in the next chapter). The number three also signifies a perfect witness to events. For example, God and his two companions going to observe Sodom and Gomorrah or Jesus taking Peter, James, and John to witness his transfiguration.

Finally, I began to think about the storage room. Why would the rabbits be in there? The original owners of the house used the room as a place to store provisions to see them through the winter. So perhaps the two rabbits in my storage room meant God was saying something about multiplying his provision for me.

When I put it all together, I came to the conclusion that God would amply provide for me that winter. Like the rabbits, I would be well fed. God would multiply my provisions, and Y2K would turn out to be as harmless as a rabbit.

Going deeper into the dream, I concluded that the lady at the door represented a mother figure in my life. That was the way I felt about the woman I saw in my dream. She was like a mother to me. So, somehow mothering was going to fit into this puzzle. God's provision would come through some kind of motherly way.

One part of the dream I still didn't get was the fact that she came through the back door. To me, something coming through the back door meant it was unexpected or not the way things were usually done. At least the back door was also an open door though, so that was okay with me.

Now the big question was, why was I angry about this "back door" provision? Sometimes you can interpret symbols right away, and sometimes you can't. That's why it is important to write things down. In this case I had to wait eight months, until June 1999, to figure it out. This dream happened while I was still pastoring at the church in October 1998. At that time, I had an income. Then, in March 1999, I quit my job. It was a difficult decision, because my position at the church was my only means of provision. I had no idea how I would support my family once I quit. Who was going to hire a burned out ex-youth pastor?

Then something amazing happened: I received news of an inheritance that was coming my way. Talk about timing! The inheritance would be enough to last me a year. I sure didn't see that coming! The inheritance began to arrive in June 1999. Isn't God's timing incredible? If it weren't for that inheritance, I would have been devastated financially.

During the ensuing year, I wanted to go back to school or get a job, but I felt the Lord telling me to wait. He wanted to give me enough time to recover from burnout before providing another ministry opportunity. When December 1999 rolled around, I had money, and enough for a good while yet. I realized this was like the rabbits—the provision I had seen in my dream! All that, and Y2K turned out to be the biggest non-story of the decade!

As my dream predicted, the money also came through a "back door," meaning it was supplied to me through a channel I didn't expect. Originally, the inheritance money was to go to my mom. She died in 1986, so her part came to my brother and me. That is why I think the Lord used a kind, motherly lady to symbolize his provision. If he had used my mother herself, I would have missed the symbolism completely, because there were too many strong emotions associated with her death. I would never have gotten past them.

Why was I angry in the dream? Truthfully, I was angry with God and angry at how my life had turned out over this time period, even with his miraculous provision. I was angry because I wanted to be working again. I had been off work for almost a year. My manhood couldn't stand it much longer! I was a good Mennonite boy, and not working was like a sin. When people asked me what I did for a living, I wanted to tell them. I wanted to be a contributor to my family's well being, to society. But the Lord told me to wait. I am smart enough to obey him but not necessarily wise enough to like it. I was angry with God, to say the least. I didn't want to be living off of my inheritance. I wanted to work or go to school.

Over time, I realized God was still trying to help me see that I could not derive my identity from what I did for a living. God wanted me to base my identity in being his son. All the same, it was difficult to accept that it was okay for me to live off God's provision. I didn't like how it looked in my eyes, and I was worried about how it looked to others. I was angry that I couldn't do anything to earn it.

Despite my anger, the image that stuck in my mind was the lady smiling at me. I told her to get her rabbits out of my house because I didn't think it was "proper." But she just gave me a smile that said, "What a cutie, he'll figure it out sooner or later." God did give me a lot of time to figure it out. He knew what my attitude was going to be like in September 1999, so he gave me the dream nearly a year in advance.

Then it occurred to me that even though God knew I was going to have a bad attitude about how he provided for me financially, he went ahead and did it anyway! That meant so much to me! It showed that he was interested in my process, not just my success. He is just as interested in your process as well.

Chapter Thirteen

SIGNIFICANT DATES AND TIMES

C*ornelius answered: "Four days ago I was in my house praying at this hour, at three in the afternoon. Suddenly a man in shining clothes stood before me and said, 'Cornelius, God has heard your prayer and remembered your gifts to the poor. Send to Joppa for Simon who is called Peter. He is a guest in the home of Simon the tanner, who lives by the sea.'*

"So I sent for you immediately, and it was good of you to come. Now we are all here in the presence of God to listen to everything the Lord has commanded you to tell us." (Acts 10: 30–33)

As Peter listened to Cornelius' story, he was looking for more of God's fingerprints. Remember: His life depended on his ability to solve this riddle! Of course, we know that God did not let him down. Recall what Cornelius told Peter about the exact time the angel appeared to him: at three in the afternoon (Acts 10:30). The timing of Cornelius' vision would have been of great interest to Peter, because the vision occurred during the third Jewish daily prayer time. (The other times of prayer being 9:00 a.m. and noon.)[1] Why is this detail significant? Because it helped Peter answer yet another prophetic question:

Do events correspond with any significant dates, such as holidays, celebrations, anniversaries or special events?

Cornelius was not a Jew and had not been converted to Judaism. He was not following the laws of Moses, and he was not circumcised. Even though he feared God, Jews like Peter would have still considered him unclean. Peter stated as much to Cornelius's face. So if Cornelius was unclean in the eyes of the Jews—and, presumably, in the eyes of God—why was God speaking to him through a vision in the same way that God had spoken to the Jewish prophets? And why did God do it according to the Jewish prayer schedule? It seemed like God was responding to Cornelius as if he were part of the covenant God had made with the Jewish people, even though all outward signs said he was not.

All of these things helped Peter to finally understand what God had been trying to tell him all along: that God did not show favoritism among races. No longer was Peter or his fellow Jewish Christians to call the Gentiles impure. Through Christ, God had made them clean. The gospel—salvation—was for everyone.

Other Examples of Significant Dates

The Bible is full of instances where God uses significant times and dates on our calendar to validate his message. The birth of Jesus during the Roman census is a good example.

> *In those days Caesar Augustus issued a decree that a census should be taken of the entire Roman world. (This was the first census that took place while Quirinius was governor of Syria.) And everyone went to his own town to register. While they were there, the time came for the baby to be born. (Luke 2:1–3, 6)*

Did you ever wonder why God wanted his Son to be born on one of the busiest dates in the Roman Empire's history? Think of how hectic it must have been. This was the first time that every citizen of the Roman Empire had to go to his or her ancestral place of birth to be registered. Imagine how many people this involved. The Romans ruled

142

over one-third of humankind. This census was an enormous undertaking. Couldn't God have picked a better time to bring his Son onto the world stage? Not a chance. This was the perfect time.

The last civil war in the Roman Empire had just been put down in Spain. For the first time in the history of the Roman Empire, there was peace. *Pax Romana* had begun—the longest stretch of peace the world had ever known. This peace meant the borders of the Empire could be clearly set and a tally of the population made. Right at this time, the moment the Roman Empire quit looking to war and started to build a peaceful empire, the King of Peace was born. Could the timing be more appropriate? I am certain that "those who had eyes to see" realized the significance of this divine coincidence.

Jesus and the Passover

As we learned in chapter three, the Passover was a special religious event instituted by God during the time of the Exodus. When the children of Israel were slaves in Egypt, God told Moses that the people should get a lamb, sacrifice it to the Lord, and smear its blood on the doorposts of their homes. Then, when the Angel of Death came, he would "pass over" these houses and leave their firstborn children unharmed. The *blood of the lamb* would protect them. Do you think it was at all significant that the crucifixion of Jesus, "The Lamb of God," took place on the eve of the Passover, the event celebrated once a year by the Jews? On the day that the Passover lamb was being slaughtered in every Jewish home in commemoration of being saved from the Angel of Death, the Lamb of God was dying on the cross so that everyone could be free from death forever. It was another perfect match.

Pentecost

When the day of Pentecost came, they were all together in one place. Suddenly, a sound like the blowing of a violent wind came from heaven and filled the whole house where they were sitting."
(Acts 2:1–4)

Today, we think of Pentecost as the day the Holy Spirit was poured out. But Pentecost was a significant day on the Jewish calendar long before this event ever happened. It was a Jewish feast that took place exactly fifty days after the Passover to celebrate the grain harvest. Do you find it at all significant that God chose this day to release the Holy Spirit?

During his ministry, Jesus compared the lost that needed saving to a great harvest. "He told them, 'The harvest is plentiful but the workers are few. Ask the Lord of the harvest, therefore, to send out workers into his harvest field'" (Luke 10:2; cf. Matthew 13, Mark 4:26–29, and John 4:35). In Acts 1:8, the resurrected Jesus also told his disciples that the Holy Spirit would come and prepare them to go out into the harvest fields of God. "But you will receive power when the Holy Spirit comes on you; and you will be my witnesses in all Judea and Samaria, and to the ends of the earth." Once again, we see that God did not pick his dates and times at random. He wanted to make sure that when the Holy Spirit came, everyone got the message loud and clear.

So it is no surprise that when Peter heard that Cornelius' vision took place during one of the Jewish prayer times, he took this as yet another indication that the vision was from God.

---

[1] For those of you keeping track of the number "3," not only did Cornelius' vision happen at 3:00, so did his subsequent meeting with Peter!

Chapter Fourteen

FROM PRIDE TO HUMILITY

By now, I'm sure Peter was a little more comfortable with the puzzle God had him working on. He had found a number of pieces: divine wordplay, timing, significant numbers, and significant dates. Yes, everything was starting to come together. However, Peter was not out of the woods yet. Not only had God brought him into a Gentile's home, possibly endangering his life, God had also told the Gentiles that Peter had an important message for them. There was just one problem: God had neglected to tell Peter what that message was. But wait! Perhaps he was finally catching on…

> *Then Peter began to speak: "I now realize how true it is that God does not show favoritism but accepts men from every nation who fear him and do what is right" (Acts 10:34).*

That's right. After hearing Cornelius' story, Peter could finally see the big picture. Through everything that had happened, Peter had gained a new worldview—a new paradigm—and Peter expressed this change using the very same words we use when we see things in a way we have never seen before, "I now realize." Finally, Peter knew why God had sent him to a gathering of Gentiles, an act that, until recently, would have meant walking away from the very God who had commanded his attendance.

Peter's paradigm had shifted from one of pride to humility. The events of the last few days had all worked together to help him see the deeper, hidden picture that God wanted to reveal. With the blinders of his Jewish tradition removed, Peter could see that God loved Gentiles as much as he loved Jews, and that Christ's offer of salvation extended to everyone. This was a revolutionary and humbling thought for someone who had probably never had a meaningful conversation with a Gentile in his life. The eighth prophetic question had been answered:

Is there evidence of a paradigm shift,
particularly from pride to humility, in the people involved?

In the course of a few days, Peter went from being a proud Jew who thought he had it all figured out to a humbled man who now had more questions than answers. Once Peter made it over this hump, however, he knew exactly what God had brought him there to say: the very same words he shared on the day of Pentecost when the Holy Spirit descended on the believers in Jerusalem. In short, he shared the gospel. He described how Jesus came to heal the sick, to make the lame walk and the blind see, how he came to set the captives free, to die on the cross and then rise from the dead, opening the way for salvation and reconciliation with God. And then Peter said these words: "All the prophets testify about him that everyone who believes in him receives forgiveness of sins through his name" (Acts 10:43). And this time, when Peter said "everyone," he meant *everyone*. Not just the Jews. This was a brand new thought arising from a brand new paradigm. Then, just in case any doubt was lingering in Peter's heart, God put the icing on the cake:

While Peter was still speaking [Right then!] these words, the Holy
Spirit came on all who heard the message.
*   The circumcised believers who had come with Peter were*
astonished that the gift of the Holy Spirit had been poured out

even on the Gentiles. For they heard them speaking in tongues and praising God. (Acts 10:44–46)

Imagine their shock: Peter and his companions were in the home of a pagan—already a bold move. But then they saw and heard exactly the same thing happen to these uncircumcised men as had happened to them on the day of Pentecost! Surely this must be some kind of mistake. Wasn't God breaking his own rules? Apparently not. But it would take some time for Peter and the rest of the Jewish Christians to sort everything out.

This was quite a journey for Peter. Over a period of a few short days, he had been forced to completely jettison his worldview. His fence of security had been uprooted and tossed away. Now he was faced with constructing a new fence in entirely unexplored territory. To think that he had just witnessed Gentiles receiving the gift of the Holy Spirit without ever having abided by the laws of Moses when a few days earlier he would not even have allowed a Gentile to eat at his table. Who would have ever thought such a thing? And if this was what God had in store for Peter when his ministry was just starting out, where was God going to take him next?

After all he had witnessed, Peter responded in a way that probably further astonished his friends, who were still picking the pieces of their shattered worldview off the floor:

> *Then Peter said, "Can anyone keep these people from being baptized with water? They have received the Holy Spirit just as we have."*
>
> *So he ordered that they be baptized in the name of Jesus Christ. Then they asked Peter to stay with them for a few days. (Acts 10:46–48)*

I'm sure Peter knew he would have a lot to answer for when he returned home. But for the time being, he was wise enough to stick around and discover all he could about what God was up to amongst his new Gentile brethren.

Chapter Fifteen

ASSEMBLING A TIMELINE

*A*s the heavens are higher than the earth, so are my ways higher than your ways and my thoughts than your thoughts.

As the rain and snow come down from heaven and do not return to it without watering the earth and making it bud and flourish, so that it yields seed for the sower and bread for the eater,

So is my word that goes out from my mouth: It will not return to me empty, but will accomplish what I desire and achieve the purpose for which I sent it. (Isaiah 55:9–11)

This passage is an excellent description of the process by which God's Word unfolds on the earth. It brings forth fruit just as rain brings forth fruit on trees and plants. But as any farmer knows, fruit does not appear all at once. Signs will begin to alert you that the fruit is on its way. First comes the budding, which is a precursor to the formation of leaves and flowers. Once the tree is in full bloom, then comes the actual fruit, which is what everyone has been waiting for. But even then, the process is not nearly complete. Before it can be harvested and eaten, the fruit must grow and ripen.

Like fruit, God's Word also follows a growth cycle. That is what God is telling us in this passage. God's Word will cause growth and change until it brings his will to fruition. It follows a timeline of fulfillment, with many signs along the way foreshadowing the harvest to come. One job of the prophet is to learn and understand this cycle, just as a farmer must learn to read the growth cycle that affects his crops. Thus, we come to our next prophetic question:

Can you organize events into a prophetic timeline?

A prophetic timeline is a series of signs and/or dreams and visions given by God that, taken together, create a single, coherent narrative. Like a good story, each prophetic timeline has a clear beginning and an ending or, as I call them, an "alpha sign" and an "omega sign." Think of alpha and omega signs in the context of a running race. A running race begins with the sound of a starting pistol and ends when the first runner crosses the finish line and breaks the ribbon. In the same way, whenever a new chapter in God's great story is about to begin, God gives us a clear sign. This alpha sign is soon followed by a number of other signs to keep us on track.

Vancouver, BC has long been referred to as "Hollywood North," because so many feature films and TV shows are shot here each year. Anyone who has driven around Vancouver is familiar with the small, brightly colored arrows that film production companies attach to streetlamps and power poles to guide their crew to a particular filming location. From the moment the crew embarks, all they have to do is follow the little arrows, and sooner or later they will arrive at the proper location. Learning to follow God's prophetic timeline is very similar. Each sign is a confirmation that we are on the right path. When God wants to say something, he will confirm his original message over and over again until we finally arrive at his chosen destination.

A Twofold Purpose

As we discussed in the previous chapter, the purpose of every prophetic timeline is twofold: To demolish lies and establish truth, to nudge us out of our false paradigm and to pull us into God's divine perspective, to move us from pride to humility. Therefore, if Peter's vision was from God, we should be able to trace these "arrows" through a complete cycle of events: first the bud, then the flowers, and then the fruit, which would be a new and improved, humbled version of the great apostle. Peter's vision was the "alpha sign." The starting pistol had gone off. After that, God sent a series of subsequent signs that all pointed back to Peter's original vision. These events were the budding and blossoming; thus providing Peter with all the information he needed to walk forward in faith, seeing life through a new paradigm.

Peter's Timeline: From Start to Finish

The apostles and the brothers throughout Judea heard that the Gentiles also had received the word of God. So when Peter went up to Jerusalem, the circumcised believers criticized him and said, "You went into the house of uncircumcised men and ate with them."

Peter began and explained everything to them precisely as it had happened. (Acts 11:1–4).

Sure enough, the folks at home were none too happy when they heard rumors of what had transpired in Peter's life over the last several days. But as Peter related the timeline of events that led to his paradigm shift, they began to have a paradigm shift of their own. From the alpha sign—Peter's vision—through to the omega sign—Cornelius and company receiving the baptism of the Holy Spirit—the council could see God's fingerprints all over the place. When Peter was finished, they could come to no other conclusion than the one Peter had arrived at himself a few days earlier. "When they heard this, they had no further objections and praised God, saying, "So then, God has granted even the Gentiles repentance unto life"" (Acts 11:18).

The Temple Falls Down in Peter's Thinking

It is important to note that during this process, Peter did not have just one paradigm shift—he actually had three! God knew he couldn't just drop a new worldview on Peter overnight. He had to ease him out of the old paradigm and into the new. Anyone who has ever worn glasses knows exactly what this feels like. You can't just put on a new pair of glasses and go about your business. It takes a few hours or days for your eyes to adjust to the new prescription. You may even suffer from a headache or nausea. Adjusting to a new paradigm is often just as unsettling.

To help Peter adjust, God had to tell his story in three acts. Crucial to this paradigm shift was reordering Peter's understanding of the temple and where the Gentiles fit into it. In fact, the temple factored so strongly into Jewish thinking that God had to remove the temple from Peter's mind entirely. In this sense, you could say that each paradigm shift Peter went through bumped the Gentiles one step closer to the Holy of Holies until, when the Holy Spirit came upon them with the gift of tongues, they were actually standing in the Holy of Holies itself—and they hadn't even washed their hands, much less been circumcised!

To summarize, here is a list of the prophetic signs God gave to Peter along the way as well as the point at which each major paradigm shift occurred:

1) Peter has his initial vision of the unclean animals.
2) The three Gentiles arrive at the gate.
3) The Holy Spirit tells Peter to go with them.
4) Peter realizes the men are Gentiles.

Paradigm shift 1: It's okay to hang out with Gentiles

5) Cornelius' vision coincides with Jewish prayer time (and the number three).

Paradigm shift 2: It's not just okay to hang out with Gentiles, apparently God accepts them.

6) The Holy Spirit falls on the Gentiles.
7) The "pagan" Gentiles speak in tongues.

Paradigm shift 3: Gentiles are on equal footing with the Jews, even without following Jewish law!

Did you ever wonder why God didn't just explain all of this to Peter and the other early church leaders straight out? Why didn't he give the New Testament church a set of guidelines to follow like he did during Old Testament times? Couldn't a voice from heaven have said, "Now boys, let's do away with circumcision. I'm sure you'll appreciate that. Also, about the temple sacrifices, we don't need them anymore. The ceremonial hand washing and ritual cleansing has also become passé." It seems strange that God never explained his will concerning the Gentiles apart from Peter's vision and experiences. It was the most important event in the history of the early Church, and God didn't say a thing about how it should be handled!

Even so, the way God handled this situation seemed good enough for the New Testament Church. Why? Because if God would have sent down a list of rules from heaven, that just would have meant being bound under an entirely new law. Little would have changed. Once again, following God would have meant following an impossible list of rules rather than re-establishing a personal relationship with our Creator.

The word "relationship" is the key to unlocking this riddle. Why did God choose to lead Peter through this rather puzzling prophetic timeline rather than dropping a new book of laws on his doorstep? Because the process he took Peter through was *relational.* What better way for God to convey his new approach to humankind than by making the process reflect the goal? To decipher God's message, Peter had to walk with God, he had to watch, he had to listen, and he had to follow by faith. Peter had to believe that God was in control of his internal dreams and visions as well as the external signs and wonders he was seeing. And, as promised in Acts 2:17–22, God used both of these realms to guide Peter into truth. Jesus had rebuked Peter for not being "up to snuff" on his symbolic language skills earlier. Obviously, Peter had done some homework since then. The promise Jesus made in John 16:12–15 about the Holy Spirit leading us into truth began to be fulfilled in the life of Peter as his obedience helped give birth to the New Testament church.

The Timeline of Jesus

"Men of Israel, listen to this: Jesus of Nazareth was a man accredited by God to you by miracles, signs and wonders, which God did among you through him, as you yourselves know" *(Acts 2:22).*

The story of Jesus is the greatest prophetic timeline God ever created. Read through the life of Christ and look for signs that accredit Jesus as the Messiah. I am sure you will find forty or more. Here is a partial list:

- The census (Luke 2:1)
- The virgin birth (Isaiah 7:14)
- Swaddling clothes (Luke 2:12)
- The star in the East (Matthew 2:12)
- The Magi and their gifts (Matthew 2:17)
- Jesus' Baptism and the descent of the Holy Spirit (Luke 3:22)
- The wedding feast (John 2:1)
- Feeding the 5,000 (Matthew 15)
- The transfiguration (Matthew 17:1–13)
- Riding into Jerusalem on a donkey (Matthew 21:7)
- Anointed for burial by woman (Matthew 26:7)
- The Last Supper (Matthew 26:17)
- The sky grows dark (Matthew 27:45)
- The earthquake (Matthew 27:51)
- The temple veil ripping (Matthew 27:51)
- People raised from the dead (Matthew 27:52)
- The Resurrection (Matthew 28)

- The stone rolled away (Matthew 28:2)
- The resurrected Christ seen by his followers (Luke 25:15ff)
- The ascension (Acts 1:9)

When Peter preached his famous sermon in Acts 2, he noted that the people were aware of these signs. All Peter had to do was tell the people what they meant. Think about that for a moment: The people in Israel had a false paradigm. They thought the Messiah was going to be a world ruler, someone who would destroy the Romans and restore Israel's sovereignty as a nation. How did God counteract this worldview? He did it by providing a series of signs that, taken together, demonstrated that Jesus was exactly the opposite of everything they expected in a Messiah. Instead of being strong, he was weak. Instead of hating others, he urged his followers to love. Instead of killing his oppressors, he allowed them to kill him instead. God used all of these signs to show the people that Jesus was his Son. Each sign was like a puzzle piece that conveyed a bit of information about Jesus' true identity.

A Final Note

Something I have not pointed out in Jesus' timeline is the alpha sign and the omega sign. Do you have any idea what these might be? Although God began foreshadowing Christ's birth way back in Genesis 3:15, it took literally thousands of years before the starting gun went off, signaling that the timeline of redemption had finally begun. Many things happened behind the scenes during that time, including the angel Gabriel's visit to Mary and her miraculous pregnancy. However, it wasn't until the night of Jesus' birth that this event really went public with the star in the East and the angel choir. I tend to think of these announcements as the alpha sign on Christ's timeline.

With the omega sign, once again we see a cluster of events that all point to the end of the chapter. There is the ripping of the veil, the resurrection of the holy people, the earthquake, the darkening sky, and then, three days later, the empty tomb. There are also the post-resurrection sightings of Jesus. But can you think of the final sign in this timeline, the one that signaled that this chapter of history was definitely over? That's right: *the ascension.* With Jesus gone, the way had been cleared for yet another age to begin. Right before Jesus went up into heaven, He hinted at exactly what this age would be—the age of the Spirit.

That brings us to another question: What signaled the beginning of this new age, this New Covenant? On what day did the starting pistol go off? Once again, you have probably guessed it already. Here is how Luke described that event:

> *When the day of Pentecost came, they were all together in one place. Suddenly a sound like the blowing of a violent wind came from heaven and filled the whole house where they were sitting. They saw what seemed to be tongues of fire that separated and came to reset on each of them. All of them were filled with the Holy Spirit and began to speak in other tongues as the Holy Spirit enabled them. (Acts 2:1–4)*

After this happened, there was no doubt in anyone's mind that a new era had begun. We are still living in the same era today, which leads to a final question: What will signal the end of this chapter? How will we know when the tape has been broken at the end of the race? Here is a hint from Matthew 24:31: "And he will send his angels with a loud trumpet call, and they will gather his elect from the four winds, from one end of the heavens to the other."

As the timeline of this age began with the wonderful sign of the outpouring of the Holy Spirit, it will end with a wonderful and dramatic omega sign. The angels will blow a trumpet, and this chapter of the Lord's history book will close. We will all get to go home to begin another wonderful epic in the Great Writer's tale.

Chapter Sixteen

HOW DOES GOD WANT YOU TO RESPOND?

A fter all Peter had seen and experienced, there wasn't much he could do besides bless it.

> *"Can anyone keep these people from being baptized with water? They have received the Holy Spirit just as we have." So he ordered that they be baptized in the name of Jesus Christ. Then they asked Peter to stay with them for a few days. (Acts 10:47–48)*

The council in Jerusalem felt the same way. Of course, they had some hard questions for Peter at first. But after they heard his side of the story, they praised God, marveling at the vastness of his grace. But they did more than that. Almost immediately, they broadened the focus of their ministry from Jews to Gentiles as well. When the Jerusalem council heard that believers from Cyprus and Cyrene had gone to Antioch and gained many converts after preaching to the Greeks, they sent Barnabas to encourage these converts and build them up in their faith. God was beginning a new work on earth, and his people partnered with him to bring the good news to all nations. We are participating in that same partnership today.

Scud or "Smart"?

During the first Gulf War, Saddam Hussein had to turn on CNN to find out where his Scud missiles had hit. The Americans, on the other hand, had "smart" bombs with cameras on them. In theory, this feature enabled bombardiers to guide their lethal payload to a precise target.

The Lord wants to reveal his plans for the earth. But few of us have developed the ability to understand him when he speaks. So many of our prayers are like Saddam's Scud missiles. Not knowing how to pray, we just fire away and hope at least one of our prayers hits its target. This is one reason why many people feel prayer is futile and overwhelming. For what do I pray, and how?

However, as we begin to ask and find answers to the prophetic questions we have just studied, our prayers become more like smart bombs, hitting their targets with laser precision. Rather than an exercise in desperation and futility, prayer becomes an ongoing adventure with God. We begin to see the Great Writer as someone who is in control, someone we can trust, and we begin to see our role as one with cosmic and eternal significance.

> *Let the saints rejoice in this honor and sing for joy on their beds. May the praise of God be in their mouths and a double edged sword in their hands, to inflict vengeance on the nations and punishment on the peoples, to bind their kings with fetters, their nobles with shackles of iron, to carry out the sentence written against them. This is the glory of all the saints. (Psalm 149:5–9)*

> *The prayer of a righteous man is powerful and effective. Elijah was a man just like us. He prayed earnestly that it would not rain, and it did not rain on the land for three and a half years. Again he prayed, and the heavens gave rain, and the earth produced its crops. (James 5:16–18)*

Blessing God's Plans/Changing God's Mind

God is speaking into our decisions as individuals, groups, and as nations every day, and he is waiting for his Bride to enter into his decisions, either by blessing them as Peter and the early Church did, or by pleading with him to change his mind. Yes, as unbelievable as it may seem, God looks for people who can see what is going on upon the earth and are willing to stand in the gap, to ask him not to pour out his judgment on the land. God wants us to cry out for mercy and ask him to grant healing and forgiveness instead.

In ancient battles, to stand in the gap of a walled city meant filling a hole that the enemy was trying to breach. Intercessors and prophetic people are called to this same duty today, to find the gaps in the walls surrounding people, churches, communities, and nations, and to plug them with prayer. We can pinpoint the enemy's target, stand where the Lord would have us stand, and cry out for mercy. The prayer of a righteous man or woman is still effective as we come boldly before the throne. This is another important role assigned to prophetic intercessors: to call down grace instead of judgment.

The book of Ezekiel contains a good example of how this can be accomplished. God informed Ezekiel and Jeremiah that judgment was coming upon Jerusalem, and he gave her people time to repent for their sin (Jeremiah 7:1–15). But the people refused to listen. So God determined that if he couldn't take the temple out of the people, he would take the people away from the temple. It was off to Babylon for everyone! Soon the armies of Babylon surrounded Jerusalem, and the city's destruction was eminent.

In the midst of the panic, Jeremiah told the people to open the gates and surrrender to the Babylonians. If they did so, they would not be harmed. Again, the people refused, still clinging to their false paradigm of how the temple would save them. The false prophets in Jerusalem supported the people in this lie. Even with God doing his utmost to save them, the people chose the familiarity of what they knew rather than the apparently risky behavior God was asking them to undertake. The result? Jerusalem was destroyed and the people were taken into captivity, just as the prophecy declared.

Was this God's heart for Jerusalem? Could things have worked out differently if God had more people praying that his will be done? Could the prayer of righteous men and women have done anything to change the outcome? Scripture definitely seems to indicate as much:

> *This is what the sovereign Lord says: woe to the foolish prophets who follow their own spirit and have seen nothing! Your prophets O Israel are like jackals among ruins. You have not gone up to the breaks in the wall to repair it for the house of Israel so that it will stand firm in the battle on the day of the Lord. (Ezekiel 13:3–5)*

> *I looked for a man among them who would build up the wall and stand before me in the gap on behalf of the land so I would not have to destroy it, but I found none. So I will pour out my wrath on them and consume them with my fiery anger, bringing down on their own heads all that they have done, declares the sovereign Lord. (Ezekiel 22:30–31)*

These two amazing passages show how the Lord was looking for someone to stand and pray on behalf of Judah, to cry out in repentance. If someone had been willing to stand in the gap, he could have refrained from pouring out his judgment. God didn't want to destroy Jerusalem. But the temple, which had been constructed to bring the people closer to God, was actually getting between God and his people. So it and the city that housed it had to go.

The Old Testament contains many other examples of holy men and women who stood in the gap and prayed for the nation of Israel, individuals who used the power of intercession to turn back the judgment of God on nations, cities, and peoples.

Numbers 14 tells us that God's anger burned against Israel in the desert. God had determined to wipe out all of Israel and start again with Moses and his family. But Moses intervened on behalf of the people and convinced God to refrain from bringing calamity. The prayers of Moses changed what God was about to do on earth.

Genesis 18:20–33 recounts how the Lord went to Sodom and Gomorrah to see if the horrible rumors he had heard about the cities were true. If they were, then God planned to wipe both cities off the face of the planet. When Abraham discovered what the Lord was up to, he interceded on behalf of the righteous people in Sodom and Gomorrah, specifically, for his nephew Lot and his family. Let's listen in on this conversation:

> *Then Abraham approached him and said: "Will you sweep away the righteous with the wicked?*
>
> *"What if there are fifty righteous people in the city? Will you really sweep it away and not spare the place for the sake of the fifty righteous people in it?*
>
> *"Far be it from you to do such a thing—to kill the righteous with the wicked, treating the righteous and the wicked alike. Far be it from you! Will not the Judge of all the earth do right?"*
>
> *The LORD said, "If I find fifty righteous people in the city of Sodom, I will spare the whole place for their sake."*
>
> *Then Abraham spoke up again: "Now that I have been so bold as to speak to the Lord, though I am nothing but dust and ashes, what if the number of the righteous is five less than fifty? Will you destroy the whole city because of five people?"*
>
> *"If I find forty-five there," he said, "I will not destroy it."*
>
> *Once again he spoke to him, "What if only forty are found there?"*
>
> *He said, "For the sake of forty, I will not do it."*
>
> *Then he said, "May the Lord not be angry, but let me speak. What if only thirty can be found there?"*
>
> *He answered, "I will not do it if I find thirty there."*
>
> *Abraham said, "Now that I have been so bold as to speak to the Lord, what if only twenty can be found there?"*
>
> *He said, "For the sake of twenty, I will not destroy it."*
>
> *Then he said, "May the Lord not be angry, but let me speak just once more. What if only ten can be found there?"*
>
> *He answered, "For the sake of ten, I will not destroy it."*

When the LORD had finished speaking with Abraham,
he left, and Abraham returned home. (Gen 18:23–33)

Wow, talk about pushing your luck! But look at how God responded! Why do you think the Lord happened to stop by to tell Abraham of his plan? He wanted someone to stand in the gap and intercede on behalf of the righteous people in these cities so his mercy could flow. God wanted Abraham to argue with him, because he wanted to know if anyone really cared. Thankfully, Abraham did argue with God, and Lot and his family were saved. God still destroyed the cities, but before he did, he gave those who were righteous a chance to get out. Once again, we see God using the prayers of a righteous man to change what he was about to do on earth.

Does God seem to be baiting you into an argument today? If so, don't be afraid to take him up on the challenge. There may be far more riding on the outcome than you realize.

Seeing Behind Closed Doors

We have looked at a few examples from Scripture where the decision made by a national leader behind closed doors affected his entire nation. Pharaoh is a prime example: Although his dialogue with Moses was carried on behind closed doors, the results of that dialogue—and Pharaoh's stubbornness—were evident for even the lowliest Egyptian to see. As I explained in chapter two, each plague struck down one of the Egyptian gods. People would have gotten the message. But would they have realized that what was going on around them was the result of Pharaoh hardening his heart and making bad decisions? Not unless they had the insight of the Holy Spirit to guide them.

What we read in the newspaper are articles dealing with events that have just been made public. Leaders who have met to discuss their plans and agendas behind closed doors have put the events we read about in motion. Usually, we only find out about such decisions days or weeks after they have been made. We do not know what was actually discussed in secret unless we are able to read God's prophetic signs, which are given long before the effects of these decisions are made public. First, the Lord listens in on the plans of men, and then he says, "That may be your idea, but this is mine. I will now send forth a series of prophetic signs so that my people may know my heart on this matter. I want my people to know of my involvement and participate in my response to your plan through prayer."

David Counts His Fighting Men

2 Samuel 24 contains another interesting tale of how things that go on behind closed doors can have grave ramifications for an entire nation. At the outset of this story, we find that the Lord was angry at Israel, so he incited David against the nation by putting it on David's heart to count his fighting men. It appears that Joab, David's commander, and some of the other army officers had a feeling this was going to turn out badly. But David overruled their objections and sent them to count the men anyway. Nine months and 20 days later, they met with David to discuss their findings. Only afterwards did David realize the foolishness of his decision.

> *David was conscience-stricken after he had counted his fighting men, and he said to the Lord, "I have sinned greatly in what I have done. Now, O Lord, I beg you, take away the guilt of your servant. I have done a very foolish thing."*
>
> *Before David had got up the next morning, the word of the Lord had come to Gad the prophet, David's seer: "Go and tell David, 'This is what the Lord says: I am giving you three options. Choose one for me to carry out against you'."*
> *(2 Samuel 24:10–12)*

David's three choices were: 1) three years of famine, 2) three months of fleeing while his enemies pursued him, or 3) three days of plague on the land. David chose "door number three," so the Lord sent a plague on Israel for the next three days, during which 70,000 people died.

When David saw the angel who was striking down the people, he said to the Lord, "I am the one who has sinned and done wrong. These are but sheep. What have they done? Let your hand fall upon me and my family." (2 Samuel 25:15,17)

This plague broke out the day after David and his army officers discussed the census among themselves and David came under conviction. The sin of the leader had affected the entire nation. How would the average Jew on the street have interpreted these events? Would they have any clue that the disease that was striking down their friends and neighbors was actually brought on by their king? Would anyone have recognized where the gap in the wall was located and/or how to fill the gap with prayer on behalf of Israel?

In this case, the only person to whom God revealed the solution was the same person who caused the crisis in the first place: David. God told him to purchase a threshing floor, build an altar there, and offer sacrifices on behalf of him and the people. When David did this, the gap in the wall surrounding Israel was filled, and the plague came to an end.

Daniel and Belshazzar

When King Belshazzar of Babylon brought out all the cups and vessels captured from the temple in Jerusalem for his guests at a party, God responded to this sacrilege by giving a prophetic sign. The hand of God appeared and wrote four words on the wall: *"Mene, Mene, Tekel, Parsin."* Unable to decipher this riddle, Belshazzar called on Daniel to interpret the message. Here is what he came up with:

Mene: God has numbered the days of your reign and brought it to an end.

Tekel: You have been weighed on the scales and found wanting.

Parsin: Your kingdom will be divided and given to the Medes and Persians

That very night, Belshazzar, King of Babylon was slain, and
Darius the Mede took over the kingdom (Daniel 5:25, 30).
Once again, we see how a rash act by a king affected his whole nation. Would the people on the street have had any idea what had caused the invasion? Would they have been watching for a sign from God? Some would have been watching for signs of God's intervention and would have responded accordingly.

Watching for the Gap and Filling It

God still reveals his plans to his servants—those that have eyes to see and ears to hear. God still wishes us to know that when he speaks with a sign on the earth, "something is up." God wants us to partner with him on earth, to find the gap in the wall by watching, and to fill it with prayer.

Svend Robinson Versus God

Let us consider a modern-day example, one in which we do not have the benefit of hindsight or a previous interpretation of events laid out for us. I am confident that we will still find the Great Author using symbolic language to alert his people to his involvement in the affairs of Man.

The case in point involves Canada's first openly gay Member of Parliament (MP), Svend Robinson. Although Svend's career ended recently due to a widely publicized shoplifting incident, for years he was a highly visible member of the federal New Democratic Party (NDP), promoting everything from gay rights to euthanasia. Throughout his career, he had numerous brushes with the law and with his opponents as he promoted his liberal agenda. We could probably trace several prophetic timelines running through Svend's life. But the incident on which I would like to focus began on December 31, 1997.

Robinson owns property on one of the Gulf Islands just off the coast of Vancouver, BC. On New Year's Eve 1997, Svend was out for a hike on his property when he fell off a small cliff, breaking his ankle and his jaw. Unable to stand because of his broken ankle and not able to call for help because of his broken jaw, Svend crawled to a neighbor's house for help.

Despite the incredible pain he experienced, Svend was able to crack a few jokes about the incident while he was being rescued, including one about the appropriateness of a politician suffering a broken jaw, seeing as politicians make their living through their ability to talk. I remember some radio talk show hosts joking about the significance of this detail as well, and I couldn't help but think, "Svend, did you ever think God might be trying to tell you something through this incident?"

A year and a half later, Svend did a very silly thing: He tried to have any reference to God removed from the Canadian constitution. Perhaps even worse was how he tried to do it.

Taking a petition that had been signed by members of his constituency, he presented his proposition before the other members of parliament during a session where no other members of his party were present. Svend had also neglected to inform anyone else in his party about his plans or to gain the approval of his caucus. In essence, Svend went behind everyone's back, probably because he knew no one else in his party would approve of the plan. As a result, when party brass heard about Svend's *faux pas,* they sent him to the backbenches.

Interesting, don't you think? Let's look at Svend's accident eighteen months earlier—the one that rendered him unable to stand or talk—and see if it may have foreshadowed this event in the House of Commons.

First, the broken jaw. Remember, this rendered Svend unable to speak. When Svend presented his petition without consulting his party, this also took away his power of speech by relegating him to the backbenches. This demotion was like getting kicked out of the inner circle, like being benched or demoted to second-string in football. Svend was no longer a player in the House of Commons; he was merely a spectator.

What could the broken ankle represent? If you think about it, Svend also lost his "good standing." Remember: Plays on words are one of God's fingerprints. As an MP serving in the NDP caucus, Svend had the right to stand up in the House of Commons to represent his constituents and his party. But Svend's deceptive behavior had cost him that right. His ability to stand up was taken away from him—because of his "slip up." Svend was no longer allowed to speak for his party or his constituency.

Here is a verse that mirrors Svend's position with striking similarity: "Confidence in an unfaithful man in time of trouble is like a broken tooth and a foot out of joint" (Proverbs 25:19). This verse essentially mirrors both physical injuries Svend suffered. This is not a coincidence. God always speaks in the context of his Word. Often, it won't be this obvious, but God's use of symbols has been consistent throughout history. Keep that in mind as you use the Bible as an interpretive tool.

Svend had proved himself to be an unfaithful man, promoting his own personal agenda by going around his own party's policies. He showed he cared more about promoting his own political goals than those of his party. In fact, his actions demonstrated that he did not trust his own party at all. As a result, not only did Svend have to face the wrath of his party, the nations' wrath fell on Svend and the NDP as well. It is kind of humorous when you think about it. Svend tried to have God removed, but God had Svend removed instead.

It would be interesting to know exactly what Svend was thinking about the night of the accident. What were his plans for the future? Was he making any New Year's resolutions? Was this plan to remove references to God from the Canadian constitution already on his heart? If so, I am certain God would have been speaking into those plans, warning him to reconsider. God never speaks into a void. In the midst of the accident, God was warning Svend to "watch his step" in the strongest way possible. If Svend had made the connection between his fall and his plans, who knows where he would be right now? Most certainly, he would have avoided the loss of reputation and career that followed.

Do you want to become a prophetic person who sees what the Lord is doing on the earth? If so, you need to discover to what the Lord is responding behind the scenes in the hallways of power. If you will become a person of the riddle and the puzzle and begin to put together what the Lord is doing on the earth, you will succeed in finding the gap and standing in it. Finding the gap takes time and research. You can do this by asking our prophetic questions and watching for the timelines of God to unfold. God will supply the pieces you need, as he did for Peter with his timeline concerning Cornelius and the conversion of the Gentiles. Once you have learned what the signs of God are pointing to, you will have found the gap to fill, and you can begin to take up your intercessory role as Moses, Abraham, Elijah, Peter, and a host of others have done.

Today, we must continue to watch and listen. How often do we ask God to bless what we are doing for him rather than seek out and follow the path he has laid out for us? Wouldn't life be more exciting if we could put puzzles together like Peter, if we allowed ourselves to be led into truth? Wouldn't it be so much better to have a new paradigm and actually see instead of stumbling about blindly in our Christian walk wondering what the will of God is or if he even has one? This is exactly what the 21st century church needs: To learn how to walk with its eyes wide open again. My hope is that as we read about how God helped people solve puzzles in the past, we will want God to help us solve puzzles today. I hope it will create a hunger to see God at work in our lives, our churches, our communities, and our nation. Let's begin to examine some of these modern-day puzzles now.

Section III

READING THE GREAT AUTHOR'S MODERN WORKS

A WORD BEFORE
WE PROCEED...

U p to this point, we have applied our prophetic questions to prophetic timelines in the Bible, particularly to the story of Peter
and his vision. Now it is time to take our newfound spiritual
eyes and train them on events that happen around us on a daily basis.

Just as he did with Moses, Ezekiel, Jesus, Peter, and countless other
people during biblical history, God is still writing prophetic timelines
today. And his purpose is exactly the same: to bring us from pride to
humility, from lies to truth. As God's people, it is our responsibility to
follow along as he writes history and to get involved where we can.

When I sense that God may be initiating a new timeline, I take out
my list of prophetic questions and begin checking off each one as it
is answered. If I only find the answer to one question, I suspect that
either I am seeing things wrongly or I am making things up. If I find
answers to two questions, I begin to look a little harder. If I find answers
to three, I usually think to myself, "What are the odds of that?" And
if I find four, five, six... well, you get the picture. The point at which
I become quite certain that God is up to something varies with each
situation. But if you find answers to half or more of the questions,
chances are good that answers to the remaining questions will not be
long in coming.

Remember: It's All About Relationship

In the previous section, I asked why God would speak to Peter using only symbolic language that was arranged into a prophetic timeline. Why didn't he just tell Peter and the rest of the early Church how to deal with the Gentiles straight out? I answered that question by explaining how deciphering symbolic language forced Peter to remain dependent on Jesus throughout the discernment process. Seeing as God's message was that *everyone* could now have a personal, intimate relationship with him, this method of disseminating the message was highly appropriate. God didn't want to give Peter mere intellectual information. He wanted to bring about divine transformation. He wanted to help Peter overcome his faulty paradigm. And, as we learned at the start of this book, the only way to get around Peter's paradigm was to speak to him in a way that forced him to jettison his old paradigm.

God works in exactly the same way with us today. He isn't interested in relaying mere information. He is seeking transformation! This comes about as we keep our eyes and ears open to what God is doing. It happens as we walk out our prophetic timelines and watch God's Word begin to bud, blossom, and bear fruit. So, with this goal in mind, let's take the prophetic questions we have developed and apply them to the Great Author's modern works.

I have applied and refined these prophetic questions while observing a number of world events over the past few years. It has been a profound joy to watch the Great Author at work as he spins new tales in his never ending story. My observations have left me with no doubt that God is in control of the affairs of men. His will, *will* be done. Watching God work has restored my confidence in his power and the insignificance of the enemy. To know this God who controls history is a wonderful thing. To know that he loves me and is intimately involved in every aspect of my life is even better. If you have any doubts about any of that, then read on.

Chapter Seventeen

CATS AND CAT-CALLS

February 22, 1999. It was time again for the yearly speech by Indian President K.R. Narayanan to the special joint sitting of India's two levels of government—the parliament and the senate. His address would be broadcast live to the entire nation so that everyone could participate in this significant event.

Although President Narayanan's role was largely symbolic—the main power rested with the prime minister and parliament—his speech at the opening of parliament was highly significant. It outlined what the government planned to do over the coming fiscal year. According to tradition, no one could speak or move until the President's speech was completed. But no one had counted on two uninvited guests who appeared in the government's midst that day. These upstarts had no intention of sitting still or listening to what the President had to say. The members of the government—indeed, the entire nation—were stunned by their antics! Nothing like this had ever happened before, and on national television at that!

Cats & cat-calls during President's speech

NEW DELHI, Feb 22: The cat crossed the Government's path this morning. During President K. R. Narayanan's speech to the joint session of Parliament, not one but two cats appeared in Central Hall and sat ominously between him and the Government MPs. They spent a full 40 minutes and by late evening, as

173

the implication of the Congress's stand on Bihar began to dawn on the Government, for the BJP it was a bad omen.

In fact, the signs were clear since morning as RLM leaders Laloo and Maulayam Yadav's were the only jarring notes during the President's speech....

It was during the concluding portion of the President's address in English that the cats parked themselves in front of Prime Minister Atal Behari Vajpayee's seat. Security personnel went into a tizzy but could do little to drive the cats out when the President was speaking.

While Vajpayee and other members of his government pretended not to notice the uninvited guests, Mulayam Singh Yadav tried several times to attract the attention of the cats. He even made a "noose" from the headphones on his desk to entice the cats who refused to budge.

The animals sat through the entire proceedings, moving about freely as security men watched helplessly. It was only after the President rose to leave and the MPs began filtering out of the central hall after him that the cats walked out too.[1]

If this were a dream, what would it mean?

Does this event cause you to ponder? It certainly had that effect on me as well as the 800-member government and the millions of people who watched the event unfold on live television. The parliamentary security men were furious. These cats were disturbing one of the most significant meetings of the year—and right in front of Prime Minister Vajpayee! The joint assembly, the very meeting that would set the tone and direction for the nation, had been hijacked by two frolicking cats!

Most telling was that even though the cats were right in front of the Prime Minister, the most powerful man in the land, he was powerless to stop them. For the full forty minutes, all the Prime Minister could do was look away and pretend nothing out of the ordinary was happening. The law forbade him or anyone else from moving during the speech. The nation of India, however, could not look away so easily.

Most people took this as some kind of sign. The question was: What did it mean? That's exactly what I was wondering about the incident. My curiosity was piqued even more the next day when I read an article in the *Indian Times* that said the Indian government had neutered both of the cats because they had embarrassed the Prime Minister on television! Out of the 800 people in the room, why had the cats decided to sit in front of him? In no time, I was digging around in the Bible to see if I could find answers to some of our prophetic questions. Would the fingerprints of God show up on an event as weird as this?

Before reading my interpretation of events, go back and read the news story again. Do some research. See how many prophetic questions you can answer. Try to adjust your eyes to the paradigm of symbolic language. Put together a possible scenario from the evidence given. Remember that the goal here is not to get this right but to gain more familiarity with symbolic language and how it works. Practice makes perfect, even when studying God's heavenly language of signs and wonders, dreams, and visions.

Do you notice any significant numbers?

When it comes to numbers, dates or any other type of symbol, the Bible is our primary source for interpretation. After digging around for a while, two numbers in particular struck me as significant in this story. Have you already guessed what they are? The first one is the number "2." *Two* cats walked into a meeting of *two* levels of government on the 22nd day of the second month (February)! Okay, sticking with our guidelines, what does the Bible tell us about the number "2"?

- "Everything shall be confirmed by two or three witness." (Deuteronomy 17:6)
- "The reason the dream was given to Pharaoh in two forms is that the matter has been firmly decided by God, and God will do it soon." (Genesis 41:32)
- "And I will give power to my *two* witnesses, and they will prophesy for 1,260 days, clothed in sackcloth. These are the *two* olive

trees and the *two* lampstands that stand before the Lord of the earth." (Revelation 11:3–4)

Other verses in which the number "2" features prominently are Deuteronomy 19:15; Matthew 18:16; Luke 9:30–31, 10:1; and John 8:17. From these examples, we can conclude that in Scripture, the number "2" speaks of a matter being decided by God and God having a witness present to observe what is about to happen.

The other significant number in this story is noted in the description of how long the President spoke and how long parliament was held powerless: 40 minutes. What does the number "40" symbolize in the Bible? As I mentioned in a previous chapter, it always has to do with testing or punishment. Here are a few examples:

> *Your children will be shepherds here for forty years, suffering for your unfaithfulness, until the last of your bodies lies in the desert."* (Numbers 14:33)

> *"I lay prostrate before the LORD those forty days and forty nights because the LORD had said he would destroy you."* (Deuteronomy 9:25)

> *"So [Elijah] got up and ate and drank. Strengthened by that food, he traveled forty days and forty nights until he reached Horeb, the mountain of God. (1 Kings 19:8)*

> *"Jesus, full of the Holy Spirit, returned from the Jordan and was led by the Spirit in the desert, where for forty days he was tempted by the devil. He ate nothing during those days, and at the end of them he was hungry."* (Luke 4:2)

Other verses in which the number "40" figures prominently are Exodus 16:35, Numbers 14:34, Jonah 3:4, and Acts 1:3. When you see the number 40, be prepared for a test to be administered. The goal of the test is to reveal what is in the hearts of the people.

Do events correspond with any significant dates,
such as holidays, celebrations, or anniversaries?

This strange event also occurred on a significant date for the government of India, the first day of Parliament, the day the President was explaining the government's objectives for the upcoming year. It appeared as if someone else was seizing the opportunity to declare his own objectives for India's government as well. A timeline from God was about to begin!

How do these events correspond to symbolic language in the Bible?

While I suspected the Prime Minister's response to the cats was the important detail here, I also knew that the cats were important in themselves. God would not choose them at random. So what does the Bible have to say about cats? Well… Nothing. However, it does give us a few hints as to how to interpret animals on a symbolic level. For instance, in Scripture, animals are referred to according to their perceived personality. Jesus called Herod a fox (Luke 13:31–32). Why? Herod was cunning, just like a fox is cunning. Or how about what Christ said about how we should be as wise as serpents and as innocent as doves (Matthew 11: 16)? Since we have looked into some of this before, I will not go on. However, it is an interesting study.

Back to cats. Some people love them, and some people love to hate them. Why? Because they give the impression of being haughty, independent, and self-serving. They act like they own the house and don't need anyone else. If you own a cat, how often does it come when you call it? Mine will—if I have the can opener in my hand. Cats are the masters of their own destiny and will not be dictated to by you, me, or even by 800 people in the Indian parliament. Keep this personality type in mind and see if it fits how the story of India and the cats plays out.

Apart from the Bible, it is also important to find out how cats are viewed in Indian culture. That's because different cultures view animals in different ways. For example, in Canada, dogs are considered "man's best friend." In Vietnam, however, "dog" is an item on the menu. Put it another way, in Canada, you walk a dog. In Vietnam, you "wok" a dog—two completely different perceptions of the same animal.

So how do Indians view cats? With a little bit of research, I discovered that Indians view cats in much the same way we view coyotes—as pests, animals not to be trusted. To get a better sense of the gravity of this event in Indian eyes, imagine how North Americans would react if two coyotes wandered into a joint meeting of the Congress and the Senate in Washington, DC and plunked themselves down in front of the President for a full forty minutes. Does the incident seem a little more shocking now?

We all know that there really is nothing wrong with cats, but Hindu's have a thing with animals. Take cows, for instance. Hindus worship them. Why? Cows provide milk and nourishment for man. What does a cat do? Cats kill the rat god, who is believed to be the constant companion of the god Ganesh, remover of obstacles and bestower of good fortune. Hence, cats are the enemy of good fortune, harbingers of doom. If God wanted to send India a message about testing or judgment, which animal would he choose? An animal like a cow that means blessing to an Indian or an animal like a cat that you can't control, an animal that, to an Indian, literally consumes their good fortune?

Do you see any evidence of colloquialisms or wordplay?

I found it interesting that the writer of this article used two colloquial expressions about cats: "cat-call" in the title and "the cat crossing the government's path" in the first sentence. If the Midianites used a common figure of speech to interpret their camp being rolled over by a barley loaf (signifying Gideon), and God used wordplay with Jeremiah regarding an almond branch, how would the Indians interpret this event through colloquial speech? Judging from these expressions, the writer of this article thinks something is rotten in Delhi. Whatever it is, it has something to do with the province of Bihar. Time for more research.

Is there evidence of a paradigm-shift, particularly from pride to humility,
in the people involved?

As I mentioned earlier, it is important to consider how Prime Minister Vajpayee and the government reacted to the cats. The government was powerless to do anything. Bound by tradition, the only option Prime Minister Vajpayee had was to ignore the cats and pretend nothing was wrong. Noting such reactions is important, because this is exactly what prophets in the Bible did. How someone responded to a sign from God revealed their hearts and instigated a response from God.

Think back to the story of Hezekiah and the Babylonian envoys. When Isaiah approached the king about the envoys, Isaiah's primary concern was not the envoys themselves but how Hezekiah had responded to them. Isaiah wanted to know this information, because the king's response would reveal what was in his heart.

Also, when Elisha told the king to strike the ground with the arrows, Elisha was angry that the king hadn't struck the ground five or six times. Why? Because striking the ground three times revealed that the king did not have a lot of vigor or passion. Striking the ground repeatedly until he was tired would have shown how much the King wanted to beat the enemy in battle. Think of it like the pre-game cheer that sports teams do before a game. If the coach shouts, "Let's go Tigers!" but all the team does is yawn, you know they are not into the game. In the same way, the king's response demonstrated that he was not in the game either. This made Elisha angry, because he knew that meant Israel would not win all of its battles. Finally, Pharaoh's response to Moses and the plagues reveals the same process. His refusal to give in determined what was coming next.

As I reviewed the article on the cats, I was struck again by the powerlessness of the joint assembly and that the Prime Minister's response to this sense of powerlessness was "business as usual." Judging from his response, I concluded that when feeling powerless, the Prime Minister tried to pretend nothing was wrong and that he still had everything under control.

Putting the Pieces Together

Let's pull together all of the puzzle pieces we have managed to gather so far. Do we have enough pieces to begin getting a sense of the big picture?

Symbolic numbers:
- The number "2," witnessed and/or decided by God
- The number "40," a time period of testing or punishment

Significant dates
- Incident took place on the opening day of parliament.

Colloquial expressions:
- Something is going on behind-the-scenes that is causing "cat-calls" or dissent in the government.
- The "cat crossed the government's path." This portends trouble brewing.
- "Has the cat got your tongue?" This definitely seemed to apply to the Prime Minister.

Biblical symbols:
- The two cats, haughty troublemakers that leave the government helpless and powerless in front of the whole nation.
- The prime minister's response revealed his heart

From these puzzle pieces, I concluded that whatever was about to happen would leave Prime Minister Vajpayee and his government powerless. I suspected that Prime Minister Vajpayee might even put up a "business as usual" façade, knowing full well that behind the scenes, things were going awry. Prime Minister Vajpayee would react to whatever was about to happen the same way he reacted to the cats. He was going to be faced with a public crisis that would leave him powerless, and he was going to act as if nothing was wrong. I thought the fact that the cats were seen by both houses of parliament and the entire nation of India meant that whatever was about to happen would also be seen by everyone. God was about to move, and Prime Minister Vajpayee and his government would be powerless to stop him.

Lastly, I considered the numbers. The number "2" signified that the Lord had made his decision and the matter was confirmed. The number "40" meant that the national government was to go into a time of testing, of being put into the balances and weighed. So whatever was coming up on India's timeline would test the character of Vajpayee and his government and reveal what was in their hearts.

Neutered

As I prayed about these puzzle pieces and how they fit together, I believe the Lord told me that however the government reacted to the cats was going to be symbolic of how God was going to react to them! Then I read that the Indian government had the cats neutered. I felt the Lord impress upon me that the Indian government would now become powerless in the two houses of parliament. They had chosen their destiny, much like the king did with Elisha when he was told to strike the ground with the arrows. The Prime Minister had chosen to harm the cats because they embarrassed him. Now the two levels of government they represented were going to politically neuter the Prime Minister.

Is there a connection between the symbolic events and events in your church, community, nation or the world at large?

I had done as much as I could with the puzzle pieces I had. Now it was time for more research. The Great Author was about to write a new chapter on India. Therefore, I knew I needed to know what God had written about the nation of India in the past so I could see how this chapter fit. What could possibly be going on in India that the Lord wanted the whole nation to know about?

Current Day India

Since this sign took place in the context of the government of India, I knew I needed to know a bit about how India is governed.

India is a democracy consisting of two houses of parliament: the *Lok Sabha,* or "house of the people," and the *Rayja Sabha,* or "Council of States." The *Lok Sabha* is elected directly by the population, and the *Rayja Sabha* is elected by the various state legislative assemblies. This knowledge will become important later on. Under the Indian system, the President is a figurehead, and the Prime Minister has the power. The Indian President has the same role as the Governor General in Canada or the Speaker of the House in the United States.

During my research, I also discovered that India has so many political parties the government almost always needs to form a coalition with other parties in order to rule. The coalition government of the moment was led by Prime Minister Vajpayee and his political party, the BJP. The BJP is based on radical Hinduism. By promoting radical Hinduism, the BJP managed to garner support by citing how religions other than Hinduism were a threat to Indian faith and culture. In their effort to remove this threat, the BJP persecuted Muslims, ripping down a Muslim mosque in 1989 that they said was built on a sacred Hindu site. Of course, this stirred up tensions, and fighting broke out between Hindus and Muslims. The Muslim population in India is quite large, and they were ready for a protracted war. Bombing by Muslim groups became a common occurrence.

It was time for the BJP to find a new scapegoat on which to blame India's problems. How could the BJP incite fear in the Hindu majority to make them band together against a common enemy? This time the BJP decided to target India's Christian community, which makes up just three percent of the population. Soon churches were being burned and missionaries killed. The main groups responsible for the killings? Two regional political parties affiliated with Vajpayee's national BJP. Once again, we see a significant number popping up: two.

The Event Behind the Event

My research turned up another significant event going on in India "right then." This event also concerned the number "2" and was partially what the article on the cats was about. It turns out Vajpayee's government had just tried to take over *two* state governments, Goa and Bihar, citing mismanagement. To understand the gravity of the situation, this would be like the federal government in Washington trying to take over the governments of California and Oregon. This was not a popular move. The takeover of Bihar was *the* hot issue in parliament the day the two cats strolled in. The Prime Minister wanted control, but the two levels of parliament and the two states of Goa and Bihar were resisting him.

Could the cats be symbolic of Vajpayee's attempt to take over these governments? All of the evidence I had gathered so far seemed to point to that conclusion. If it was the Lord, then Vajpayee was going to be rendered powerless in his attempts to control these two state governments. If this did not happen, then my search would be over. It was time to watch events unfold.

Can you organize these events into a prophetic timeline?

If this was the Lord, then God's Word had to bud, then blossom, and finally produce fruit. Everything that was about to happen had to fulfill the original sign of the two cats, just as everything that happened after Peter's vision fulfilled what the Lord had told him. Would the pieces of this puzzle continue to fit? Let's have a look.

President's rule in Bihar revoked

NEW DELHI, March 8, 1999: The President's rule in Bihar was revoked tonight paving the way for the restoration of the Rashtriya Janet Al (RD) government, which was dismissed on February 12.

The order revoking the imposition of central rule was signed tonight by the President, Mr. K. R. Narayanan, a Home Ministry spokesman said.[2]

When I watch events into which I think the Lord is speaking unfold, usually the next stop on the timeline is confirmed within a short period of time. Notice the date in the article above. It was written approximately two weeks after the cat incident. During the intervening two weeks Vajpayee's government began to crack. If the government in a parliamentary democracy tries to pass a resolution but is voted down, that is taken as a non-confidence vote in the ruling government, forcing an election. As this article reports, Vajpayee's attempt to take over Bihar was voted down in parliament by some of the people in his own coalition. The cracks were beginning to widen. Vajpayee's coalition was falling apart behind the scenes. He was losing control of the national government. And things were about to get worse.

AIADMK ministers resign

NEW DELHI, April 6, 1999: Two AIADMK ministers in the union ministry, Mr. M. Thambidurai and K.M.R. Janardanam, today submitted their resignations to the Prime Minister, Mr. Atal Behari Vajpayee.

The ministers' resignation follows a directive from party supremo J. Jayalalitha in the light of the rejection of her three demands by the Union Cabinet on the Bhagwat-Fernandes issue.[3]

It was now a little over a month after the incident with the cats. Vajpayee's coalition government had spent the entire time holding back room discussions aimed at holding the government together, apparently to no avail. Therefore, the event described above was no surprise to me. I had been expecting something that might destabilize the government. Seeing the number "2" pop up again here added incentive for me to watch and pray.

As it turned out, Vajpayee's majority would stand or fall on the votes from these two members of parliament. If they walked away from the coalition and voted against the government, the government would fall, and a national election would be called. The leader of the two resigning members' party, J. Jayalalitha, had been trying to cut a deal with Vajpayee behind the scenes. She had Vajpayee right where she wanted him. If Vajpayee didn't do as she said, she could bring his government down by removing her two MPs.

Just as the alpha sign had portended, Vajpayee was now powerless. This powerlessness was evident for all to see as the two MP's mocked him to his face and took control of his government's destiny. As he did during the cat incident, the Prime Minister tried to pretend nothing was wrong, acting as if it was business as usual.

Government will survive, says PM

BATESHWAR, April 6, 1999: Prime Minister Atal Behari Vajpayee today asserted that his government would survive the present political crisis and sought "everyone's cooperation" in overcoming the same.

Addressing a public meeting at his birthplace, Mr. Vajpayee said "some persons are creating problems for the government, which completed one year recently. But all challenges will be overcome and the country's interests safeguarded."[4]

This did not sound like someone who was about to lose control of the country. And yet the two MPs had neutered Vajpayee and his government. It is important to note here that Vajpayee's government did not hold the majority in the Council of States. Now it appeared that it would also have no power in the Council of the People. Neutered in both legislative bodies. And, just like the incident with the cats, the entire nation of India was watching.

India's prime minister expected to resign
after government loses confidence vote

NEW DELHI, April 17, 1999: Prime Minister Atal Bihari Vajpayee was expected to submit his resignation Saturday, after his crisis-plagued government fell, when it lost a vote of confidence in parliament by a single ballot.

The count vote was 269 votes in favour of a motion express-ing confidence in the coalition led by Vajpayee's Bharatiya Janata Party, and 270 votes against. The number of abstentions was not announced.

Vajpayee convened a cabinet meeting after the vote.

"The result of the division is ayes 269, noes 270. Noes have it, noes have it, noes have it," speaker Ganti Balayogi declared after a second ballot was held to clear up doubts over the verdict of the initial, electronic vote.

The vote, which followed two days of debate and frantic maneuvering for support by parties on both sides, was always on a knife edge. But on Friday it appeared the government might have won just enough support to survive the vote. [5]

Slightly less than two months after the two cats had crashed parliament, Vajpayee's government collapsed. To win this vote, Vajpayee required the two ballots cast by the two MP's who quit his party. The crisis that Vajpayee had tried to pretend wasn't there had overtaken him. After all the back room meetings and negotiations, the Prime Minister turned out to be powerless. The crisis in his government, which he pretended didn't exist, had now neutered him—just as he had neutered the two cats. His voice had been removed from the political halls of India, and the nation of India saw the whole thing play out on their television sets, just as they did with the cats. What are the odds of that?

As an aside, it is quite interesting how often the number two emerges in this timeline. Just for fun, let's look at how many times it shows up:

• Two radical Hindu parties, the BD and the VPD
• Two houses of government
• Two states taken over
• Two cats walk in
• Date of joint assembly: Feb 22
• Two MPs quit the coalition
• Vajpayee loses by two votes

- Two days of debate
- Loss on second ballot
- The entire timeline took roughly two months to complete

Are you convinced yet that God may have had a hand in these events?

Summary

Here is a quick summary of events, illustrating the main events and the symbols that foreshadowed them:

Symbol	Thing symbolized
Two cats	Two states, two levels of government, 2 MPs
40 minutes	Time of testing/punishment
Vajpayee ignores the cats	Vajpayee ignores his political problems
Vajpayee neuters the two cats	Vajpayee and his government are neutered politically
Vajpayee rendered speechless by cats	Vajpayee's loses his voice in parliament
Vajpayee embarrassed publicly by cats	Vajpayee and his government embarrassed publicly

The mere fact that these two cats could wander in to a nationally televised gathering of leaders on one of the most significant days of the political year was amazing in itself. But it is absolutely astounding that in a matter of two months, the events that the two cats foreshadowed came true.

Hindsight

Yet again, we have seen how God's timeline unfolded to display what he was up to. It was all there on display so that God's church, we who read his modern works, could follow along and get involved. I took this as yet another reminder of the need to watch and pray.

However, I still had some questions. When elections were finally held a year later, the BJP were voted back into power. Why, after all that had happened? What was the Lord up to?

Part of the reason for this episode, I think, was to break Vajpayee and his government's pride. God removed Nebuchadnezzar from power for the same reason and then reinstated him when he had learned his lesson. Maybe God wanted to teach Vajpayee and the BJP a similar lesson, that they couldn't take over regional governments without accountability. Maybe he wanted to show Vajpayee and the BJP that they couldn't pick on God's people, the Christians. Either of these answers could be correct. But I believe the real reason is this: God wanted to show the people of India what their leaders were made of. He wanted to reveal their hearts.

God has revealed the hearts of people like this before: He gave the people of Israel a forty-day test when Moses was on the mountain. Fearing that Moses had died, they turned to a golden calf to lead them instead of turning to God. The people failed the test and nearly paid for it with their lives.

The children of Israel underwent another forty-day test when the spies went into the Promised Land but came back with a negative report. They failed that test, too. The Lord responded to the people based on their response to the test, acting in accordance with the desires of their heart. The people did not want God's blessing, so he did not give it to them. Rather than enter the Promised Land, they were forced to wander around in the desert for forty years until nearly every person in that generation had died.

In the case of India, I believe God was testing the people to see whether they would back a man who abused minorities and threatened to set off nuclear weapons in the name of Hindu pride or whether they would choose other alternatives, such as Mrs. Gandhi's Congress party, which had ruled India for over thirty years. After being given another chance like this, you think people would be a little more careful.

I believe that whatever is coming down the road for India, the Indian people have chosen it for themselves. No longer can they stand before the throne and say, "Lord we never had a chance." The Lord will say, "Yes you did, but you decided to take this road—you voted for it as a nation—and you will reap what you have sown." But the story of India is not over yet. In fact, only recently, Mrs. Gandhi's party was voted back into power. Thus, we and the people of India must continue to watch and pray.

[1] "Cat and Cat-calls During President's Speech," http://www.indiaexpress.com/archive_ frame.php (February 23, 1999).

[2] "President's Rule in Bihar Revoked," http://www.tribuneindia.com/1999/99mar09/ (March 8, 1999).

[3] "AIADMK ministers to resign," http://www.tribuneindia.com/1999/99apr07/ (April 6, 1999).

[4] "Government Will Survive, Says PM," http://www.tribuneindia.com/1999/99apri07/ head.htm#3 (April 6, 1999).

[5] "India's Prime Minister Expected to Resign After Government Loses Confidence vote," http://edition.cnn.com/WORLD/asiapcf/9904/india.01/index.html (April 17, 1999).

Chapter Eighteen

FIRE IN THE CASTLE

It Was the Worst of Times...

Annus Horribilis. That is what Queen Elizabeth called it, the horrible year: first one, then another, and finally, the beginnings of a third divorce. The whole world watched the self-destruction of the Royal Family on TV and read about it in the morning papers.

It all began in March of 1992 when Prince Andrew and Fergie announced their intention to divorce. The following month, Princess Ann divorced Captain Mark Phillips. By summer, the whole world knew of Princess Diana's secret phone calls to James Gilbey. Although the nation could see the problems in Charles and Diana's marriage, the palace made no comment until November 6. On November 13, the press released excerpts of a lurid phone conversation between Charles and his mistress Camilla.[1] And then—seven days later, on the Queen's 45th wedding anniversary—came perhaps the worst disaster of all:

Fire Damages Windsor Castle

LONDON, November 21, 1992: Fire swept through the ornate rooms of Windsor Castle on Friday as the Queen and the Prince Andrew helped remove art treasures from her weekend residence.

A distressed Queen assessed the damages as more than 225 firefighters fought a blaze that began at about 11:30 a.m. in a private chapel in the castle's Northeast wing.

She helped carry treasures out of the castle, a royal residence for the past 900 years.

The fire continued to burn Friday night, thick smoke billowing out of the towers windows, and orange flames licking at ramparts around the 1,000-room castle, west of London... [2]

The article goes on to say that the fire was particularly destructive, because the private chapel where it started was in the centre of the building, connecting many areas together. This enabled the fire to spread in all directions.

By the time the fire trucks roared onto the scene, it was no longer safe for firefighters to access the building. Eventually, crews made the difficult decision that parts of Windsor Castle would have to be sacrificed to save the whole. In the end, the fire burned for fifteen hours before firefighters brought it under control.

The Queen was in shock. How could such a horrible thing happen in the midst of all the personal tragedy she and her family were already experiencing? It didn't make any sense. Surely there was a greater likelihood that the castle would have burned in previous centuries, not today with all of their modern fire prevention devices. And why now, on her anniversary?

If this were a dream, what would it mean?

This was the first prophetic question that entered my mind. I would never presume God to be the cause of the fire, but was he speaking to us from within its flames? Was the Great Author using the fire to draw our attention to the fact that he was about to end the current chapter in his story of the British monarchy and begin a new one? Could we find answers to our prophetic questions in this event and the ones that followed?

192

The View of the People, Past and Present

The fire's symbolism was not lost on the people of England. Over the centuries, they had come to view Windsor Castle as a symbol of the monarchy itself. With so much strife in the Royal Family, it did not take a rocket scientist to see that the monarchy seemed like it was about to crash and burn just like their castle. Divorce, gossip, bitter public disputes between members of the Royal Family, even dissatisfaction among the nation toward the Royal Family's tax-exempt status. The British people knew the monarchy was in trouble. The fire at Windsor Castle seemed to portray exactly what the people already thought and felt as they watched Queen Elizabeth and her family.

Is there a connection between the symbolic events and events in your church, community, nation or the world at large?

I was able to find several articles that made these sorts of connections. For example:

> *This palace within a castle has been occupied by the Royal family for at least 800 years. In that way Windsor Castle, and particularly this corner of it, is more than merely a symbol of the crown's immense depth of continuity; these buildings are the physical embodiment of it. In many ways, nowhere in the country is richer, either historically or symbolically. Chance had it that it was here that the disastrous fire of 20 November 1992 broke out.*[3]

Another publication noted,

> *The Royal Family has strenuously denied that Windsor Castle is symbolic of the British monarchy. But that is precisely what a succession of British sovereigns—notably Edward III, Charles II and, most spectacularly of all, George IV—intended it to be, its magnificence a reflection of the power of crown and country. That was certainly how the world saw it as the smoke and flames billowed upwards on the night of Nov 20, 1992—as yet another*

symptom of the annus horribilis, the worst year for the monarchy since the Abdication.[4]

Symbolic connections ran rampant. The *Sunday Telegraph* quoted a line from Edmond Burke written after the French Revolution:

As long as the British Monarchy, like the proud keep of Windsor girt with the double belt of it's kindred and proud towers, as long as these endure, we are all safe together, the high from the blights of envy, the low from the iron hand of oppression."[5]

This quote is particularly interesting, because Burke linked Windsor Castle and its fortunes to the British Monarchy almost 200 years ago. This view had changed little in the minds of the British people. But the common people were not the only ones who regarded Windsor Castle as a symbol of the monarchy. As the second article above suggests, Windsor Castle was built and redesigned by succeeding monarchs specifically to reflect the power and stature of the Royal Family. Now both the Royal Family and the castle that represented them were on fire with the whole world watching. In fact, Diana had told one of her friends, "The symbolism of the fire at Windsor Castle was not lost on anyone inside the (royal) family." [6] What were the odds of that?

Something was going on. Christians and non-Christians alike were drawn into a state of pondering, making connections between the fire and the goings-on in the Royal Family. One question that probably divided Christians from non-Christians at this time, however, was this:

What does God want me to do in response?

Merely making the connection was not enough. The only reason the Lord would want us to understand what he was up to would be to encourage us to begin praying according to his will. But what did he want us to pray for specifically? Did he want us to bless what he was doing or urge him to reconsider? To answer this question, I needed to look at this fire and other current circumstances on a deeper level, to see the picture within the picture. It was time to ask more prophetic questions and seek out God's prophetic timeline.

If this were a dream, what would it mean?

Let's return to this question. One way of answering it is by considering an additional question: When the people of Great Britain thought of Windsor Castle, what did they picture? This will help us get at the symbolic significance of the building and the fire.

William the Conqueror began the work on what is today Windsor Castle back in AD 1066. Unlike most castles across Europe, Windsor Castle is not an historical museum but a royal residence. It has been in continual use for almost 900 years, making it the oldest, continually used castle in the world. In addition to serving as a Royal retreat and residence, Windsor Castle is used for official functions such as entertaining foreign heads of state and the Ceremony of the Garter (during which the Queen confers knighthood upon worthy citizens). The castle also houses St. George's chapel, home to more than a few royal weddings and church functions. From this brief review of history, we can see that Windsor Castle is symbolic of:

1) The Royal Family, in their political role as head of state
2) Rest and repose, in the castle's role as royal residence and family home
3) The Royal Family, in their religious role as Head of the Church of England (indicated by the Private Chapel as well as Saint George's Chapel)[7]

In short, Windsor Castle represented the Royal Family in all their varied roles to the people of Great Britain. What would a fire in this potent national symbol represent? It was time to look for more puzzle pieces.

How do these events correspond to symbolic language in the Bible?

If the symbolic meaning of fire in the Bible did not connect the troubles in the Royal Family with what is going on in their castle, I knew my journey had come to an end. This was a very tall order, but I was about to see it filled.

Fire in the Bible

In Scripture, fire typically represents testing and the presence of God. It burns up whatever is not holy, whatever is not built upon the things of God. For example:

> *For no one can lay any other foundation other than the one already laid, which is Jesus Christ. If any man builds on this foundation using gold, silver, costly stones, wood, hay or straw, his work will be shown for what it is because the day will bring it to light. It will be revealed with fire, and the fire will test the quality of each man's work. If what he has built survives, he will receive his reward. If it is burned up he himself will suffer loss; he himself will be saved, but only as one escaping through the flames. (1 Corinthians 3:11–15)*

Other scriptures that reference fire in this fashion are Genesis 19:24, Isaiah 66:15, and Hebrews 12:29. Fire tests what we have made. It tests our character to see if we are like Jesus. It reveals our lack of morals and integrity. It is the fire of God's holiness, for our God is a consuming fire (Deuteronomy 4:24).

Knowing this, would it be reasonable to assume that there were some things going on behind the scenes with the Royal Family upon which God's fire of judgment had been released? Definitely. Moral failure, adultery, and lack of integrity nearly always reap the fire of God in Scripture. So it seems like we have a match between the symbol of fire in the Bible and what is going on in the Royal Family. This brings us to our next prophetic question:

196

Do you see any evidence of divine timing?

Five days after the fire, Charles and Diana sat down and agreed to separate.[8] How close to the date of the fire might they have made that difficult decision in their hearts? I'm only speculating, but it would not be totally preposterous to suggest that the decision to separate may have come on or about the day of the fire.

In fact, friends of Charles and Diana recall that it was the weekend of the fire that their marriage came apart.[9] This bit of information is important; because, as you will remember, when God gives a sign, he usually does so in response to what is taking place behind the scenes, not in response to events that are already public knowledge. Granted, by the time of the fire, most people knew that the Royal Family was falling to pieces. But the fire indicated there was still more going on behind the scenes, things that hadn't yet made the papers. The odds that the fire spoke into Charles and Diana's decision to separate were very high.

Is the private chapel important?

The fire in Windsor Castle started in the private chapel, supposedly by a light that was touching a drape. Even though the light had been in that position for years, it had never caused a problem. Investigators concluded that since the light was left on for a longer period than normal while work was going on in the castle, this somehow started the fire. It was an educated guess, but the best they could come up with after examining the smoldering wreckage. In other words, the source of the fire was rather... puzzling.

If the private chapel is a puzzle piece, it is important to know the purpose of a private chapel. What would a private chapel mean to someone? What would they think about when they were inside? On what occasions would someone visit such a chapel?

The purpose of a chapel is to meet God and to make commitments, such as wedding vows, child dedications, baptisms, communion, and so forth before God and other people. Could the fact that the fire started in the Royal Family's private chapel have any significance in this regard? In other words, if a chapel represents making vows of commitment, might the fact that the fire started in the private chapel in Windsor Castle symbolize some kind of break in the Royal Family's commitment to God and each other, particularly in the area of wedding vows? Knowing what I did of the Royal Family at the time, it certainly sounded plausible. First, wedding vows were broken, and then the chapel that symbolized wedding vows burned down. I also knew that fire represented the judgment of God on sin. Once again, I thought I had a match.

Do you see any evidence of colloquialisms or wordplay?

In Scripture, we find David's family line called the "House of David." Saul's family line is referred to in a similar fashion as the "House of Saul" (2 Samuel 3:1). Why do I mention this? Because this is where I ran into the first play on words. The Royal House of Windsor has just been devastated by fire. Windsor Castle is referred to as a castle because of its size, but it is a house nonetheless, because it is a royal residence. At the same time, the "House of Windsor" or Royal Family, also has a fire break out in its midst, in the form of divorce. Thus, the fire at Windsor Castle became a prophetic play-on-words. The physical fire in Windsor Castle depicted the spiritual fire in the House of Windsor. God's judgment had fallen on the sins of the Royal Family. It was purging time. The holiness of God had burned up the dross, and the House of Windsor had been found wanting.

Do events correspond with any significant dates, such as holidays,
celebrations, or anniversaries?

As we have already noted, the fire occurred on the Queen's 45th wedding anniversary. This was a time for the Queen and the entire Royal Family to focus on the institution of marriage. It was also a time to look back at where they had come from and to look ahead to where they were going. Once again, it appears as if God had appropriated a significant date on the human calendar for his divine purposes. He does this so that people can see what he is up to, to underline or draw special attention to his actions. He was speaking into the context of people's experience, trying to tell them that he was about to begin a new era for the British monarchy as well as the British nation as a whole.

One final note on this prophetic event: Windsor Castle was not destroyed completely; it was merely gutted. That means it did not have to be abandoned completely, but it did need to be rebuilt. If the fire in Windsor Castle represented God's fire of judgment and purging on the Royal Family, then the results of the fire should also match up. Just as Windsor Castle was remodeled and updated, I knew I should see evidence of this same process happening in the Royal Family. God was going to purge the monarchy and bring it up-to-date.

The Puzzle Pieces Add Up to the Big Picture

Looking at all of the puzzle pieces I had gathered, this is how things had come together: Judgment and purging from God began when members of the Royal Family broke their marriage vows. The House of Windsor had entered a season of testing, judgment, and purging. The Royal Family needed to be remodeled and updated. God had initiated this process in response to the belief systems and lifestyles of the monarchy. How does this sound so far? Not bad, but now it was time to ask the big question:

Can you organize these events into a prophetic timeline?

If God has spoken, then things will change (Isaiah 55:9–11). It was time to begin watching for that change, to see what God's Word would produce. Soon, I would know if the fire at Windsor Castle was a sign from God or if I was merely reading a spiritual interpretation into what could possibly be a random event, an act of carelessness that led to calamity. But if God really were at work behind the scenes, then his Word would accomplish what it was sent out to do. So I decided to review our criteria briefly to see how things were going:

1) Just as the prophets of old pondered events, I had begun to ponder the fire at Windsor Castle as a possible sign from God.

He may not have caused the fire, but I was convinced he was speaking from its midst to the Royal Family and to the people of Great Britain.

2) I had also found a clear connection between the symbolic event—the fire—and current events in the Royal Family, most notably, all of the marital discord.

3) The symbolic meaning of the fire also seemed to line up with the symbolic meaning of fire in Scripture, which is usually "judgment" or "testing."

4) The timing of the divorces and the fire was indisputable.

5) I had found evidence of colloquialisms or wordplay.

6) The fire occurred on a significant date in the life of the reigning monarch.

Six of our prophetic criteria had been fulfilled. So far, so good. But now that I had a possible interpretation of events, I needed to test it. The way to do that was to see if I could assemble the puzzle pieces into a prophetic timeline of confirmation that would produce what such prophetic timelines always produced in Scripture: humility and a new paradigm. Otherwise, I had to assume my reading of events was inaccurate.

A Caveat

It is at this point that many prophetic people get off track. Many times when we hear God speak or see something that we are certain is a sign, the excitement of discovery leads us to force an interpretation. We lean on our own feelings or understanding. But we need to remember that it is not our job to come up with the answers; it is our job to watch and listen to what the Holy Spirit is saying. These prophetic questions are biblical tools to keep us moving so we can be guided by the Holy Spirit while at the same time staying on the right road.

Keep in mind how we have seen some of the timelines in the Bible work out. Peter's timeline began with a vision. Peter recognized his vision as the first puzzle piece and then proceeded to work with the Holy Spirit to assemble subsequent puzzle pieces into a prophetic timeline. Peter's vision was proven accurate not because of his own understanding but because of the way the timeline unfolded afterwards. I was at the same point as Peter was. My interpretation of the Windsor Castle fire could only be proven accurate through the unfolding of events that would come together to form a coherent timeline. For this to be the Lord, the events would have to match my hypothesis. Otherwise this could all be a figment of my imagination. Peter's timeline ended with a new paradigm that allowed the Gentiles to become part of the kingdom of God. How would the Royal Family's timeline end?

Watching the Timeline Unfold

The restoration of Windsor Castle was now underway. All of the burned out guck was being exposed and removed. Amazingly, this same process was going on inside the Royal Family as well. All of the guck that had been going on behind the scenes was being brought to the surface for the entire nation to see.

Article after article containing accusations and counter-accusations made by members of the Royal Family was published. With the fire of judgment came the exposing of sin. Much of the fighting was linked to the divorce of Prince Charles and Princess Diana. Remember how many books about Diana came out over those years? As the accusations piled up, Diana finally decided to share her side of the story through a television interview. Her decision had devastating results, especially for Prince Charles. According to one poll conducted after Diana's interview, more than one-third of respondents said they thought less of Prince Charles after the interview than they did before it. A large percentage of Britons even thought the Royal Family should skip a generation and let Prince William succeed to the throne.

All the years of behind-the-scenes scandal and infighting had taken their toll. Great Britain was losing faith in its monarchy, or at least in their next monarch. The people wanted the monarchy to change. Some even wanted the monarchy to leave.

The fire in the Royal Family had done its job. Everyone, the Royal Family included, knew things had to change. So the Queen set out on a new course designed to drastically alter what the Royal Family was all about. The Queen realized it was time to remodel the monarchy. The old ways of thinking had to go. No longer could the past dictate the future.

Downsizing The House of Windsor

NEW YORK, Aug 25, 1996: Queen Elizabeth II's father, George VI, once remarked that British royals are "not a family, we're a firm." Like any sensible CEO under fire, the Queen has formed a "Way Ahead" committee to reconsider the firm's vision as it heads into a new century after a series of troubled years.

Under discussion are ideas for radically altering the crown's source of income, scrapping it's role of defender of the faith, ending male primogeniture, downsizing the size of the Royal family itself and dropping the ban on marriages to Roman Catholics. The committee, consisting of the Queen, her consort, all their children and palace advisers, is committed to discussing these ideas.

The reforms seem a rational response to the outcry, including calls for abolishing the monarchy, resulting in the messy public dissolution of Prince Charles' marriage to Princess Diana.[10]

It must have been extremely stressful for the Queen to sit in meetings and discuss remodeling the way the Royal Family had always done things while all around her the castle that represented the Royal Family was being remodeled.

Out of the Frying Pan…

Change was in the air for the House of Windsor, but things would get worse before they got better. We all remember the fateful night of August 30, 1997 when the car that was carrying Diana and her companion Dodi Fayed crashed into a Paris underpass, killing Diana, Dodi, and their driver.

The people of Great Britain realized that Diana had tried to bring change to the Royal Family, but the Royal Family had resisted. Many believed it was this resistance that indirectly led to Diana's death, one of the most publicized events of the last century. The people of Great Britain were angry at Diana's needless death, and they placed the blame at the feet of the Royal Family. The English people were beginning to lose confidence in the Royal Family. Now, with its brightest star gone, support for the Royal Family dipped even lower. The Royal Family's response to Diana's death did not help matters any. They left London and disappeared from sight, didn't lower the flag, and didn't express the emotion that the nation felt. The nation was in pain, but the Royal Family that represented them did not seem to care. The people were incensed. For the first time in the history of the Royal Family, almost half of Great Britain was leaning toward the idea of abolishing the monarchy.

Wow, Great Britain without a monarchy. Who could imagine such a thing? Apparently, more and more people had no problem with the idea. In fact a senior palace source confided later: "We nearly lost it."[11] But then came the Queen's response:

The Queen bows to her people

LONDON, *February 25, 1998: The Queen is to address the nation following criticism that has caused profound distress to the Royal Family. She will also travel to London today to pay her private respects at the coffin of Diana, Princess of Wales, and meet mourners at St James's Palace.*

At 4pm, she will record a message of sorrow and condolence. The broadcast—the idea of the Prince of Wales—will be transmitted later today. It has also been announced that the Union flag will fly at half-mast on Buckingham Palace, for the first time, during and after the funeral.

There had been complaints that the absence of the Queen from the capital and a flag from the Palace showed disrespect to the Princess. Such remarks were attacked yesterday by the main political parties and the Church.

The Queen's decision to break family mourning at Balmoral a day early follows grave concern by the Prince of Wales that criticism from certain sections of the public and the media was threatening the dignity and solemnity of tomorrow's funeral.

In another departure from tradition, the Queen authorized her press secretary, Geoffrey Crawford, to appear before television cameras to express the Royal Family's pain at the attacks of recent days.[13]

The Turning Point

I included the previous article for a couple of reasons. First, I believe the title of this article is a prophetic statement describing what the Queen was compelled to do as a result of Diana's death. To bow in Scripture was to submit to someone greater, to humble yourself before someone else, because they didn't owe allegiance to you, you owed allegiance to them. Diana's death was like a deathblow to the old ways of the monarchy. The monarchy had expected people to bow to their will. Now the monarchy had to bow to the will of the people. It was time for the monarchy to stop asking the people to serve them and to start serving the people instead.

Tradition vs. Progress

As the article mentions, much of the public furor focused on the flag not being lowered to convey the country's sense of loss. To be fair, the reason the flag wasn't lowered for Diana's death was due to tradition, not negligence. The flag was *never* lowered at the death of a Royal Family member, not even for the King or Queen. That's because in the traditional British way of thinking, the flag represents the monarchy and the nation, not any particular monarch. Even though individual rulers or

Royal Family members may die, the monarchy lives forever. It had been that way for hundreds of years. Nevertheless, the people of Great Britain were no longer content with this tradition. The Royal Family's refusal to lower the flag came to represent the crux of the problem Great Britain had with its monarchy. It revealed to the people that, once again, the Royal Family had chosen tradition over them. The battle over whether or not to lower the flag for Diana revealed to the nation that the Royal Family was out of touch with the hearts of their own people.

The people were also angry that the Queen and her family had left London and gone into isolation. They did not address the nation or reveal any emotions publicly in regard to Diana's death. Thus, it appeared that the Royal Family did not care. Once again, however, what the people were observing was not lack of concern but strict adherence to tradition and heritage. According to tradition, mourning the death of another royal was a private affair. The monarchy was supposed to have a "stiff upper lip" to model the strength of the nation. The monarchy's role was to inspire the people, to model how the people should be. But now the people were demanding a "touchy-feely"[13] monarchy, a monarchy that reflected the mood of the nation rather than projecting how they should be. For perhaps the first time in their history, the Royal Family had to choose between the will of the people and the tradition passed down through the generations.

Diana's death brought the nation's dissatisfaction with the Royal Family to a focal point. "Change or become obsolete" was the cry, and it jarred the Queen into seeing how out of touch with society she had become. The Queen heard the people, and she bowed to their will. The monarchy would begin to listen to the people and represent who they were, not who they were supposed to be. The nation of England had been undergoing a paradigm shift in regard to the monarchy for some time. Now, at this critical moment, the Royal Family had finally caught up.

Do you notice any significant numbers?

On November 20, 1997, five years to the day after the fire, the renovation of Windsor Castle was complete. Windsor Castle had a new look that managed to keep the best of the old while upgrading for the 21ˢᵗ century, as the following articles note:

New look Windsor for the new look monarchy

LONDON, November 17, 1997: Restorations have been completed at Windsor Castle, after more than 100 rooms were destroyed by fire five years ago....

The fire, on November 20, 1992, was the final blow to Queen Elizabeth's "annus horribilis," which saw the serial breakup of her children's marriages.

The Queen has described the restoration as "a wonderful anniversary present" as she celebrates 50 years of marriage to Prince Philip this week... [14]

A Vigorous Blend of Old and New

LONDON, December 27, 1997: The renovation, finished six months ahead of schedule, was completed just in time for a 50th wedding anniversary dinner and ball in November for the queen and her husband Prince Philip.

"It is a mixture of the original with later additions and alterations... the result, a vigorous blend of the old and the new," the queen said in her Christmas message. [15]

The number "5" in Scripture often represents grace (Lev 1-5, Eph 4: 11). The year of Jubilee in Scripture took place every 50 years. During this time, all debts were to be cancelled and all slaves released. People began anew. This is exactly what happened to Windsor Castle and the House of Windsor on the Queen's own Jubilee, a new beginning.

If Windsor Castle represented the monarchy, and now the castle had been restored, how about the monarchy that the castle represented? Had it been restored as well? How was my timeline doing?

As it turns out, the re-opening of Windsor Castle was not the only significant event of November 20, 1997. This day was also when the old ways of the monarchy died and the Queen promised the British people a modernized, remodeled monarchy.

Queen promises to modernize the monarchy

LONDON, November 20, 1997: The Queen has marked her Golden Wedding anniversary with a promise to listen to public opinion and adapt the monarchy for the future.

In a speech to mark the occasion, she said the hereditary monarchy, like the Government, existed only with the support and consent of the people.

She was speaking at a banquet hosted by the Prime Minister, Tony Blair—a gathering dubbed a "people's banquet" because so many "ordinary people" were invited as guests....[16]

Is there evidence of a paradigm-shift, particularly from pride to humility, in the people involved?

Five years to the day of the fire, on the very day that Windsor Castle was reopened, on her 50th wedding anniversary, the Queen indicated she would listen to her people. Another incidence of divine timing! To prove her point, the Queen held a banquet that included ordinary people like policemen, nurses, businesspeople, and others with whom no king or queen had ever associated. Those who demanded that the monarchy change had been granted their wish. The Queen had truly learned humility and was beginning to walk in a brand new worldview. She had begun to relate to ordinary people—not as someone who demanded allegiance but as someone who sought to encourage those around her. It truly was a "new look" monarchy for a "new look" Windsor Castle. Shortly afterwards, the Queen actually went into a pub to meet more ordinary people. No monarch had ever done that! Her way of relating and the rules regarding to whom she could relate were changing daily.

Winds of Change Blow Through the Nation

Windsor Castle had been remodeled, and the Royal Family had made a profound paradigm shift, "You don't serve us, we serve you." But was that all? Could the fire at Windsor Castle have been symbolic of more than just the Royal Family? Could the new paradigm achieved by the Royal Family extend to Great Britain itself?

Britannia

For centuries, Britain had a naval empire that spanned the globe. The royal ship *Britannia* was a stirring symbol of that naval empire, for it indicated that the Queen of England ruled from sea to sea. It used to be said that the sun never set in the British Empire, because their empire spanned two-fifths of the globe. *Britannia,* the Queen's ship, was a symbol of that rule. It had been that way for centuries. A ship named *Britannia* had always represented the Empire and the Royal Family. Not anymore. This important national symbol was about to bow out of existence. By the time Windsor Castle was restored, *Britannia* had been mothballed. In late October 1997, the *Britannia* set sail for its farewell voyage around Britain. The previous summer, the ship also steamed out of Hong Kong's harbor on June 30, 1997, thus lowering the curtain on Britain's rule of that colony and returning it to Chinese control. Many Britons felt a twinge of sadness as the people of Hong Kong returned to China, but the Queen was keen to take a positive view. She said, "We should be proud of the success of our partnership in Hong Kong and in *how peacefully the old Empire has been laid to rest.*"

Government

During the five years of radical change in the House of Windsor, the prophetic winds from heaven changed everything they touched in Great

Britain. This change solidified with the election of Prime Minister Tony Blair. Look at his comments below. Keep in mind the article about a "New Look Castle for a New Look Monarchy." The sub-head of that article was "A Vigorous Blend of Old and New." Both Windsor Castle and the monarchy tried to keep the best of the old and move on to the new. Now the government of the United Kingdom was going to do exactly the same thing within the same five-year time span.

An Interview With Britain's Prime Minister

LONDON, October 27, 1997:

TIME: Britain has voted for political change, but isn't this country also searching for something more?

Blair: Absolutely. I thought that the minimum that people wanted was a change in government. But in fact people were on to something far bigger than that. The victory is an expression of the fact that a new generation has come on that doesn't have the outdated attitudes of the past. There is a curious mixture of optimism about the future mixed with a realization that the old British ways of getting things done are not going to be enough. There is a tremendous sense of confidence in the country today, and it comes from having found out what our role in the world is....

We cannot pretend that the Empire is back because it isn't. My generation has moved on beyond all that. My generation has come to terms with its history. When I see the pageantry in Britain I think that's great, but it does not define where Britain is today. The whole idea of a modern British identity is not to displace the past, but to honour it by applying its best characteristics to today's world.

The important thing to realize is that what I call the new British identity isn't about displacing all your past. It's about saying that the country has an exciting future and that we have different attitudes today, but there are bits of our past we are delighted with. [17]

In essence, the Prime Minister of England was saying that the people of England had undergone a paradigm shift. They elected him and his government because they realized the old ways weren't working anymore. It was time to remodel Great Britain, and remodel is exactly what Tony Blair did.

Not Nation Building But Nation Releasing

The week before he gave this interview, Tony Blair met with Gerry Adams, leader of Sinn Fein, the political arm of the Irish Republican Army. Blair was the first Prime Minister in seventy-six years to hold such a meeting. The goal of this get-together was to initiate a plan for self-government in Northern Ireland. As astounding as this event was, it was but one of many similarly astounding events during those five pivotal years of reconstruction.

In September 1997, Britain gave Wales its own parliamentary assembly. This was the first measure of self-rule granted to the region since AD 1283. England had stifled Wales as an independent people for over 700 years. Now, at this critical juncture in history, things were about to change. Freedom was coming as Britain remodeled what they were and what was important to them.

Also in September 1997, Britain gave Scotland its own parliamentary assembly as well. I am sure you have seen the movie *Braveheart*. This portrayed the battle of independence waged by the Scots against England until 1707, when the Scots lost the right to self-rule. It was time for this to change, for Scotland's relationship with England to be remodeled. It was also the end of the book on the British Empire. However, a new book on Great Britain was just beginning.

Consider what a monumental paradigm shift this was and how many people it impacted! Britain went from a nation that demanded allegiance to one that permitted freedom at its own expense. This was evident in the Royal Family, in parliament, and among the common people. As the Royal Family remodeled their relationship with the people of Great Britain, so England remodeled its relationships with its former colonies and territories. Tony Blair was right: The people of England had let go of their outdated attitudes. They wanted to keep what was good from the past and blend in the new.

Epilogue

The fact that such a fire took place and the whole nation saw it as symbolic was amazing. To see the wholesale change in the House of Windsor that followed was astounding. To see the British Empire swept away, for the Welsh and the Scots and the Chinese people in Hong Kong to be given freedom after hundreds of years within the same five-year timeframe was staggering. And all of this was reported extensively in the news for everyone to see. The clues that God was at work were waiting out in the open. God was telling a story about the destiny of one of the greatest empires the world has ever seen. Could the British Empire have gone the way of the Roman Empire and died? Absolutely. That is what happened to most other monarchies in Europe. But the signs from God spoke otherwise, and the signs proved true. God had something different in mind for the British monarchy.

The question is, how many people in England saw God's hand at work? Many recognized that their country was going through massive change, but how many knew beyond a shadow of a doubt that all was going to be set right because the sovereign God had declared it so? How many took comfort in God speaking through these events? How many partnered with him during this time, urging him to forestall judgment and bring about redemption instead? How about you? Did you recognize any of this at the time?

Great Britain's Prophetic Timeline—From Start to Finish

This has been quite a journey. Let's summarize all that has gone on:

- March/April 1992: Princess Ann divorces Captain Mark Phillips; Prince Andrew divorces Sarah Ferguson

- 1992: Prince Charles' affair with Camilla Parker-Bowles becomes public knowledge.
- November 20, 1992: Fire at Windsor Castle; Queen's 45th wedding anniversary
- December 1992: Charles and Diana legally separate
- 1993–1995: Public in-fighting in the Royal Family, leading to Diana's fateful interview with the BBC, where she admits to having had an affair and accuses the Royal Family of being uncaring. This is the last straw for the Queen, who demands that Charles divorce her.
- 1995: Public opinion of Prince Charles begins to wane
- July 1996: Charles and Diana divorce
- August 1996: Queen begins downsizing and remodeling the House of Windsor
- Summer 1996: Push to complete the restoration of Windsor Castle
- May 1997: Tony Blair and Labor Party form Government of Britain
- June 30, 1997: Britain hands Hong Kong back to China
- August 31, 1997: Diana dies in a car wreck in Paris
- September 1997: Public outcry against Royal Family's response to Diana's death; First Welsh parliament since AD 1283; first Scottish parliament since AD 1707
- October 1997: *Britannia* decommissioned
- November 20, 1997: Queen's Golden wedding anniversary; Restoration of Windsor Castle is completed five years to the day of the fire; Queen promises remodeled monarchy

As you can see from this case study, the Great Author still loves to spin a good tale. He also still speaks the same language, the language of signs. This language is available for all of us to read, if only we will take the time to watch, learn, and enter in to what the Great Author is doing.

[1] "The Princess and the Press," http://www.pbs.org/wgbh/pages/frontline/shows/royals/etc/cron.html/.

[2] "Fire Damages Windsor Castle," *The Vancouver Sun,* November 21, 1992, p. A15.

[3] Nicolson, Adams. *Restoration: The Rebuilding of Windsor Castle.* (London: M Joseph Ltd.,), 1997, p. 4.

[4] "On Her Majesty's Service," *Electronic Telegraph,* Jan 31, 1998.

[5] *Restoration: The Rebuilding of Windsor Castle,* p. 70.

[6] Andrew Morton, *Diana, Her New Life* (New York: Simon and Schuster, 1994), p. 57.

[7]The Queen is the head of the Church of England just as the Pope is the head of the Catholic Church in Rome. This all has to do with a dispute between Henry VIII and the Pope, so you can look that up if your interested.

[8] Lacy Robert, *ROYAL* (London: Bettenham House, 2002), p. 328.

[9] Tim Clayton & Phil Craig, *Diana: Story of a Princess.* (New York: Pocket Books, 2001), pp. 243–244.

[10] "Downsizing the House of Windsor," *New York Times,* August 25, 1996, pp. 4, 12.

[11] "The Changing Face of the Monarchy," http://news.bbc.co.uk/1/hi/special_report/1998/diana/59991.stm (February 25, 1998).

[12] "The Queen Bows to Her People," http://www.telegraph.co.uk/htmlcontent,html=archive1997/09/05/indi05.html (September 5, 1997).

[13] "The Changing Face of the Monarchy," http://news.bbc.co.uk/1/hi/special_report/1998/diana/59991.stm (February 25, 1998).

[14] "New Look Windsor for New Look Monarchy," http://news.bbc.co.uk/1/hi/32057.stm (November 17, 1997).

[15] "Windsor Castle Reopens Five Years After Devastating Fire," http://edition.cnn.com/WORLD/9712/27/windsor.castle/index.html (December 27, 1999).

[16] "Queen Promises to Modernize Monarchy," http://news.bbc.co.uk/1/hi/uk/33290.stm (November 20, 1997).

[17] "Compassion and "hard Choices" An Interview With Britain's Prime Minister," *Time Magazine,* October 27, 1997 Vol. 150 No. 17.

Chapter Nineteen

SWISS TRAGEDY

No survivors in Canada air crash

LONDON, September 3, 1998: Swissair says there are no survivors from the airliner that crashed into the Atlantic Ocean off the eastern Canadian province of Nova Scotia.

In a statement, the airline said, "All 215 passengers and 14 crew members died in the crash."

The McDonnell Douglas MD-11 was en route from New York's John F. Kennedy Airport to Geneva when it plunged into the water at night.

Local authorities said the weather in the area had been good, with clear skies and relatively calm seas...[1]

Most likely you remember hearing news reports like this one just over seven years ago. You probably also remember the hundreds of people who flocked to Peggy's Cove, Nova Scotia from around the world, hoping against hope to find their loved ones still alive or simply seeking closure.

Of the 229 people who died in the crash, 136 were American citizens. The remainder included thirty French, twenty-eight Swiss, six Britons, three Germans, three Italians, two Greeks, and single passengers from Saudi Arabia, Yugoslavia, Afghanistan, Iran, Spain, St. Kitts, and Russia.

Between six and ten United Nations officials were among the dead, as was one high-ranking World Health Organization official.

Upon first glance, there doesn't appear to be anything profoundly prophetic about this accident. It was just plain tragic. However, my interest was piqued when it was followed shortly by a second tragedy, also involving the Swiss. You may remember this story as well:

Swiss ambassador crushed by train: Diplomat was returning to Ottawa from Switzerland with his wife

OTTAWA, September 6, 1998: Ottawa's diplomatic community was in a state of shock last night upon learning that Switzerland's ambassador to Canada was killed yesterday when he fell into the path of an oncoming train in a southern Swiss town.

Daniel Dayer, 58, had been waiting on the platform at the train station in Sion when he apparently tripped in front of an oncoming Brig-to-Geneva train travelling at 35 km/h. He was killed instantly. Police have launched an investigation into the accident.

Swiss embassy spokesman Martin Bienz said Mr. Dayer's death has taken a heavy toll on embassy staff who are still dealing with the crash of Swissair Flight 111 that killed all 229 aboard the MD-11 plane.

"We were still in shock from the airplane crash so now for this news is just terrible," Mr. Bienz said. "He was very sad when (the crash) happened. It was tough for him because he was not in the country when it happened." [2]

Again, on the face of things, this seemed like just another tragedy. But, taken together as a unit, the two tragedies seemed to indicate something was up.

If this were a dream, what would it mean?

What are the odds of the Swiss Ambassador to Canada, who happened to be in charge of dealing with the political and emotional fallout of the Swissair 111 crash, being killed within three days of that catastrophe? Two related events happening within days of each other is usually a sign that something is up. Experience has taught me that whenever God speaks prophetically, there will often be a witness, a second confirming sign. I began to see this second event with the Swiss Ambassador as evidence that a gap had opened up in the spiritual wall around Switzerland. Somehow the enemy had gotten into the camp. God wanted to draw his servants' attention to this breach so they could fill it with prayer.

Finding God in the Midst of Tragedy

God has good reason for us to watch and pray in the midst of such events. We have an enemy. Actually we have two enemies: 1) the devil, who wants to destroy humankind, and 2) the sinfulness of humankind itself, which leads us to cooperate with the enemy and get ourselves into trouble. Both of these enemies invite the judgment of God on the earth. The problem is, with two enemies it is often difficult to know which one we are fighting when! This is quite a dilemma. If God gives us signs, such as the Swissair crash, and in the midst of those signs people die, how do we respond? Do we say it was the enemy and attribute power to him? Or do we say the event was the judgment of God on sinful man and make God out to be an egotistical killer? How do we find the heart of God in the midst of this situation? The answer to this dilemma is found with Jesus and his heart for Jerusalem.

> *"O Jerusalem, Jerusalem, you who kill the prophets and stone those who are sent to you, how often I have longed to gather your children together, as a hen gathers her chicks under her wings, but you were not willing.*
>
> *Look, your house is left to you desolate. For I tell you, you will not see me again until you say. 'Blessed is he that comes in the name of the Lord.'" (Matthew 23:37–39)*

This passage took place right before Jesus' dissertation on the signs of the end of the age in Matthew 24. While Jesus spoke of these things, he was grieved and heartbroken. Jesus wanted to protect Jerusalem, but he knew it was too late. The people had chosen a future that did not include redemption, and it broke his heart.

Even though Jesus knew Jerusalem wouldn't listen to him, he didn't leave it at that. Jesus sought to protect his followers by telling them how to read God's sign language concerning the destruction of Jerusalem so they would see it coming and get to safety. Some of the signs Jesus mentioned in Matthew 24 include:

- Many people claiming to be "the Christ"
- Wars and rumors of war
- Nation rising against nation
- Kingdom rising against kingdom
- Famines
- Earthquakes
- Persecution and death
- People falling away from their faith
- False prophets deceiving people
- An increase in wickedness
- Love growing cold

Scary stuff. Why do you think Jesus chose such horrible signs to signal his return? The answer is simple: Jesus didn't pick the signs; Man did. Jesus was only working with the options he had left. Jesus wanted to save everyone in Jerusalem. If Jerusalem would have accepted him and ditched the false paradigm of the Old Covenant, he would have been able to do so. But the Jews chose to reject Jesus instead. That decision set in motion a series of events that culminated in the destruction of the temple in AD 70.

Destruction was coming on Jerusalem, so Jesus alerted his followers to a number of signs that would let them know when it was time to get out. The signs began to accumulate, and the Christians began to watch. Agabus predicted the famine in Acts 11:28–30, and Paul and Barnabas were sent to Jerusalem with relief. Earthquakes also struck the cities of Phrygia, Laodicea, Hierapolis, and Colosse.[3] History records that when the Roman army surrounded Jerusalem, they originally lifted the siege and left. Upon seeing this sign, the Christians realized this was what Jesus had told them to watch out for, so they left the city before the Roman army returned.[4] Keep in mind that in those days, when people saw an army coming they would flee *into* the city so they were safe behind the city's walls. The Christians, however, appeared to be running the wrong way! That's because they remembered what Jesus had told them to watch for. Many of the signs from Matthew 24 and Luke 21 that scare us actually saved the Christians' lives. Maybe that is why Jesus said: "But when you hear of wars and commotions do not be terrified" (Luke 21:9) and "Now when these things begin to happen, look up and lift up your heads, because your redemption is drawing near" (Luke 21:28).

The signs of destruction were not God's choice, but he was willing to work in the midst of what Man had chosen to save his followers. God wanted to save everyone, but only those who were willing to watch and pray would be saved. "And what I say to you, I say to all: Watch!" (Mark 13:37).

We find this same pattern with Ezekiel concerning Jerusalem and the temple. God asked the nation of Judah to do what was right and to serve him, but the people would not listen. So, in the midst of the destruction that followed, God placed a number of signs that would alert those with eyes to see and ears to hear that, if they would trust and obey him, God would deliver them from calamity.

Even in the midst of tragedy, the hand of God never quits working for redemption. This was true in Ezekiel's time, and it is true today. We may have stopped listening, but that doesn't mean God has quit trying to get his point across, to save us from devastation. This help comes in the form of signs, like that found in the midst of the Swissair crash, which indicate how the enemy got into the camp and how to fill the gap so he can't get in again.

The plane crash, followed closely by the death of the Swiss ambassador, led me to believe that some kind of shift in the spiritual realm had taken place, something to do with the leadership of the country. God's hand of divine protection had lifted for some reason. There was a gap in the wall. What had caused the gap; and how could we work together with the Swiss to fill it?

Investigating the Crime Scene

I re-read the articles on the plane crash and the death of the ambassador as sign language, as if the events were dreams that spoke symbolically of bigger things. Specifically, I was searching to discover what the following elements represented:

- The plane
- The people
- The crash
- The ambassador
- The ambassador's stumble
- The train

To involve both the national Swiss airline and the ambassador of Switzerland, I knew God was trying to draw our attention to something fairly major, probably involving the entire nation. Therefore, as I studied each component listed above, I knew I needed to research what was going on in Switzerland at the time and see how these components might represent those events.

Is there a connection between the symbolic events and events in your church, community, nation or the world at large?

Often in a dream, a vehicle represents the direction in which some aspect of our lives is going. The bigger the vehicle; the bigger the direction and/or purpose. In this case, the vehicle was quite large—a jumbo jet—and the owner of the plane was Switzerland. Therefore, I speculated that something big was crashing in Switzerland.

But what was this exactly? Did we have any more specific information? I took a closer look at the article on the plane crash. Maybe the Lord would release other clues so I could intercede according to his will.

The Function of the Plane

One detail of the Swissair crash that struck me was that the plane was carrying people from all over the world. If the plane represented the nation of Switzerland, then the people on that plane should represent something Switzerland carries for the world.

As I pondered what this could be, I concluded that it would have to be banking, cheese or chocolate. I doubted that the cheese or chocolate industries would be important enough to be connected to such tragedy, so I decided to focus my research on international banking. Just as the Swissair flight was carrying passengers from all over the world, so the Swiss banking system carries the finances of people from all over the world.[5] The Swiss handle banking on an international scale. Therefore, I conjectured that the Swissair plane might represent the Swiss banking system. Was it about to crash? If so, why?

The Ambassador

To gain an understanding of what the Swiss ambassador might represent, it was important for me to know what an ambassador is and does. I discovered the job of an ambassador is to represent his or her nation to other nations of the world. Thus, it seemed obvious that the Swiss ambassador represented the Swiss government, particularly their involvement with the plane crash. And, if the plane crash represented a crash in the Swiss banking system, then the Swiss ambassador probably symbolized the Swiss government's response to that crisis.

Do you see any evidence of colloquialisms or wordplay?

I didn't like where this was leading. If the Swiss ambassador slipped and died on the way to deal with the plane crash, what did that say about what would happen to the Swiss government as they sought to deal with the banking crisis?

You are probably familiar with the saying "slipped up," which means to make a mistake or a wrong decision that costs you in the end. If the Swiss ambassador represented the Swiss government, then the ambassador's slip-up probably meant the Swiss government would slip up in its response to the banking crisis.

The Train

Since I already knew that vehicles typically represent the direction and speed in which a person, organization, community or nation are going, I guessed that as they were on the way to deal with this banking crisis, perhaps the Swiss were run over by someone else's agenda. Maybe another nation or group of people were involved.

Putting all the Puzzle Pieces Together

This was still all conjecture, of course, but I felt confident that if something were going on, it would likely be along these lines. Therefore, as the puzzle pieces emerged, my interpretation of events went as follows:

Symbol	**Thing Symbolized**
Swissair plane	Swiss banking system
International passengers on Swissair	International money invested in Switzerland
Swissair plane crash	Crash in Swiss banking system
Swiss ambassador Swiss ambassador on his way to crash	Swiss government Swiss government on way to deal with deal with banking crash

Swiss ambassador "slips up"	Swiss government "slips up"
Swiss ambassador hit by train	Swiss government "railroaded" by someone else's agenda

In summary, I believed these two incidents pointed to an imminent crisis in the Swiss banking industry. The Swiss government would try to fix the problem, but they were going to handle it poorly. This error would cost them big time, and another nation was going to punish them for it.

Again, this was all still conjecture, possibly the product of too much pizza the night before followed by a strong coffee buzz. However, I would be able to find out if my interpretation had any credence merely by watching events unfold. Something would be evident around the time of the plane crash. On or around September 3–5, something must have occurred in the spiritual realm that allowed the enemy to come in and steal, kill, and destroy. Whatever that event was, it would have been reported in the media. All I had to do was find it. Was anything going on in the Swiss banking industry that was significant enough to fit my interpretation of these two possible signs? Had the Swiss government dropped the ball while trying to intervene in some kind of bank scandal? It was time for more research.

The Swiss, The Holocaust, and Nazi Gold

It did not take much searching before I discovered a huge international crisis in the Swiss banking industry. It turned out that every bank in the nation was being audited. That's right, the most secretive banks in the world had to open up their records and let accountants from all over the world see what they were hiding! Nothing like that had ever been done before! What were the odds of that?

The international audit was being carried out due to suspicions that Swiss banks were hiding gold that belonged to Jews who were killed by the Nazis in World War II. Prior to the war, these Jews had stashed their money away in Switzerland, but they never returned to claim it.

That was not the worst of it. As time went on, it was revealed that the Swiss were actually acting as the Nazis' bankers,[6] conducting 79 percent of their gold transactions.[7] Some of that gold was taken from the teeth of murdered Jews then melted down and shipped to Switzerland for safekeeping. Despite these gruesome details, rather than releasing the money and gold to relatives of the deceased, the Swiss banks held onto it for themselves. One particular bank circulated a memo stating,

> *In the case of inquiries about Jewish clients whose assets had to be transferred to Germany in the 1930's, we have always responded that we could not supply the requested information, because we are only obliged to retain ledgers and correspondence for ten years.*[8]

Another memo found in the same bank stated that the bank could "skim off" the interest earned by such money and recreate the account documentation as if no profits had been earned. Such illegal and immoral practices had been going on for some 60 years, earning nearly $7 billion for the banks involved.[9]

Change Begins

In 1996, a young security guard named Christophe Meile who worked at the United Bank of Switzerland was instructed to burn some ledgers dating back to the 1930–40s. Meile believed the banks were breaking their own laws by burning their old ledgers. These laws stated that any bank account records relating to possible Holocaust survivors be saved and used to help identify heirs. Meile decided to sneak some of these ledgers out of the bank and take them to a Jewish congregation in Zurich. Little did he realize how significant his actions would become.

When the news broke, the United Bank of Switzerland accused Meile of theft. He even received death threats, forcing him to flee the country. But by July 1997, the United Bank of Switzerland finally admitted it had broken the law. Meile demanded to know why it took them so long to admit it and why they harassed his family. When asked why he took the ledgers, Meile replied, "I did the right and moral thing. I am a Bible-believing Christian and regard Jews as my brothers."[10]

The story doesn't end there. The international uproar set off by Meile's find put so much financial pressure on the Swiss that they had to open up all of their bank records from the war era. An international team of accountants was called in to go through all bank records pertaining to that time period to see if any Nazi gold was hidden away from Jewish clients. This commission, called the Virkler Commission, brought in 500 accountants to go through approximately four million accounts in fifty-nine banks. On November 19, 1996 the Swiss banks' Ombudsman Hanspeter Haeni reported that he had found only $8,800 belonging to heirs of the holocaust. The World Jewish Council was furious with this outcome. They believed there was upwards of $7 billion in those same accounts. But they would have to wait for the outcome of the Virkler Commission's investigation to be sure.

How Does It All Fit?

This was all very interesting to say the least. However, I did not see a clear connection to the Swissair crash or the Swiss ambassador's death. The crisis in the Swiss banks began in May 1997, but the plane crash did not happen until September 3, 1998. It was a little disheartening to get so close and then to have the dates not match up. For this to be the Lord, I knew we would have to see more evidence of divine timing. I decided to see how the Swiss government was involved in the banking scandal in and around the time of the Swissair crash. If the Swissair plane crash and the death of the Swiss ambassador had any symbolic meaning, something had to have happened with the Swiss government and its banks on or near that date. Perhaps some behind the scenes meeting or decision had been made, thus precipitating the prophetic signs I was seeing.

Switzerland Breaks Covenant

Upon doing more research, I discovered that the World Jewish Congress, the World Jewish Restitution Organization (which represents Jews of eastern European descent), the Swiss commercial banks, the Government of Switzerland, and the Swiss National Bank were trying to negotiate a settlement. The Swiss group was offering $600 million, a far cry from the original $8,800 they said was present in the accounts. Meanwhile, the Jewish organizations were asking for $2 billion. They had reached a stalemate. In July 1998, several American states began preparing sanctions against all Swiss banks, both national and commercial, that would potentially cost the Swiss billions of dollars. These sanctions, which were like a starting pistol signaling the beginning of a timeline, were to go into effect on September 1, 1998—*two days prior to the Swissair crash and four days prior to the ambassador's death.*

*Do events correspond with any significant dates, such as holidays,
celebrations or anniversaries?*

The Swiss went ballistic when they heard about the sanctions but agreed to a $1.25 billion settlement package. The Jewish organizations accepted the Swiss offer, and it looked like everything would end nicely.

Suddenly, the trail appeared to be getting thin. In fact, I was beginning to think I had walked down a long, albeit fascinating, rabbit trail. A happy ending would neither incur the judgment of God nor reveal a gap in the spiritual wall surrounding Switzerland, meaning my interpretation of events was completely off. I was stumped, but I decided to dig a little deeper.

The Plot Sickens

With the deal in place and all parties apparently on board, the threat of sanctions was dropped. Then, suddenly, the Swiss government changed its game plan. During the last week of August 1998, the Swiss government and the Swiss National Bank (the equivalent to the U.S. Federal

Reserve Bank or the Bank of Canada) backed out of the deal and refused to sign the document.[11]

With the sanctions set to be lifted, the World Jewish Congress, U.S. Senator D'Amato and the other groups involved vowed to fight on.[12] They believed that the Swiss National Bank and the Swiss government should be held accountable for their crimes.[13] However, there was no longer enough international pressure to force the Swiss government back on board. It appeared that the Swiss had played a pretty good hand of poker, bluffing their way out of having to pay up.

Why was this such a big deal? The Swiss National Bank, not the commercial banks, held the majority of that Jewish gold. According to 1940s figures, the Swiss National Bank had an estimated $280 million while the commercial banks held just $56 million. Converted to today's values, both banks were holding billions of dollars illegally. This was also a big deal to the Jewish groups, because they wanted the Swiss government and the Swiss National Bank to declare their guilt for this financial boondoggle publicly by being a part of the holocaust settlement.

Neither the government nor the state bank was willing to do this, and that is why they refused to sign the deal. This stance flabbergasted the World Jewish Restitution Organization and those working to bring a settlement:

> *"Particularly upsetting is the role,"* asserted Hevesi, *"not of the banks so much, but as the Swiss government and the Swiss National Bank, two thirds of the problem is their problem and they refuse to acknowledge and sit down and participate in, as I say, moral and material restitution."*[14]

Because of this treachery, a dispute developed between the Israeli and Swiss governments. The Swiss accused Prime Minister Benjamin Netanyahu of flagrantly supporting the efforts of the Jewish National Congress during the negotiations.[15] A prominent Swiss government official even cancelled his pending trip to Israel, which was to be made in mid-September. Netanyahu responded by canceling his own plans to visit Switzerland in early November.[16] As a result, mid-August through to the middle of September was a time of great tension between the Jews, the nation of Israel, and Switzerland. Smack in the middle of this mess we have, you guessed it, the plane crash and the ambassador's death. I hate to sound like a scratched CD but… What are the odds of that?

What's the Deal about the Deal?

Why is all this important? Because the Swiss government and the Swiss National Bank made a deal with the Jewish people and then reneged when the pressure was off. [17] I believe that by doing so, they invited the judgment of God upon themselves. They slipped up, stepped out from under God's protection and opened themselves up to the enemy's attack. Consequently, God released signs in the midst of this tragedy to reveal what was going on and, hopefully, find someone to stand in the gap for Switzerland through prayer.

Remember: This deal was not just about the money. Of course the Jews wanted Switzerland to give back the gold and any profits they had made from it.[18] But perhaps even more than that, the Holocaust victims wanted the Swiss government to apologize for colluding with the Nazis and to admit they were wrong. On January 1, 1997, Jean-Pascal Delamuraz, who at that time held the rotating position of President in the Swiss government, said, "This is nothing less than extortion and blackmail. This fund would make it much more difficult to establish the truth. Such a fund would be considered an admission of guilt."[19]

When the pressure of sanctions and world opinion were against them, the Swiss government backed away from President Delamuraz's earlier position. But with the pressure off and no one to hold them accountable, the Swiss government and the Swiss National Bank refused once again to sign the settlement, stating that signing the deal would "lend this an official character, which is not in the interests of the country as a whole."[20] The Swiss government and the bank refused to admit they had done any wrong, a prideful false paradigm, to be sure. But God always resists the proud. That's what his paradigm-busting symbolic language is all about.

228

Do you see any evidence of divine wordplay?

Everything seemed to be lining up. We were looking for a date near September 3–5 1998, something that was happening behind the scenes with the Swiss government and the Swiss National Bank. The event had to show evidence of the Swiss "slipping up" in their response to the banking industry. It also needed to show that this slip-up led to the Swiss being railroaded by another group's agenda. I stumbled across an interesting quote while researching this piece that shows the position in which the World Jewish Congress, U.S. senator D'Amato (who was leading the investigation), and their team of lawyers and strategists found themselves in when the Swiss government and the Swiss national bank refused to be a part of the agreement:

> *The Swiss government refused to join the talks. Hevesi and McCall were committed to their self-imposed deadline of September 1. Eizenstat was out of negotiations and the WJC (World Jewish Congress) had seen enough of Swiss stalling tactics. This scenario had all the markings of the unavoidable, as they say in Washington, of an "impending train wreck." Meanwhile, within the disparate group of lawyers a "train wreck" was about to occur as well.*[21]

What an interesting metaphor for the banks not signing the deal and the fallout that would occur once the sanctions were set to begin! I had found this whole "train wreck" analogy through the story about the Swiss ambassador being hit by a train. What are the odds of that?

I was looking for something of such significance that it would bring about the judgment of God and open a gap in the wall for the enemy to enter. Miraculously enough, I had found an event that seemed to match our criteria almost perfectly: the Swiss government and national bank breaking the deal.

How do these events correspond to symbolic language in the Bible?

Now it was time to go back to Scripture and find out the results of breaking a deal or "covenant" made in good faith. During the reign of

David, there was a famine for three successive years; so David sought the face of the Lord. The Lord said, "It is on account of Saul and his bloodstained house; it is because he put the Gibeonites to death" (2 Samuel 21:1).

This was a strange tale. The Gibeonites were a foreign nation that lived among the Israelites. They were Amorites by heritage and had come to serve Israel by tricking Joshua into signing a treaty with them after the defeat of Jericho. Israel did not consult the Lord before signing the deal, so they fell for the ruse. Only three days after making the treaty and having their elders ratify it by oath did the Israelites learn that the Gibeonites were actually their neighbors. As a result, "The whole assembly grumbled against the leaders, but all the leaders answered, 'We have given them our oath by the Lord, the God of Israel, and we can not touch them now'" (Joshua 9:15–16,19).

Why do you think that the leaders of Israel refused to go back on their word? Because they knew breaking the deal would invite God's judgment. This seems strange, seeing as the Gibeonites didn't bargain in good faith. But a deal is a deal. This particular deal was upheld all the way to the time of Saul, who broke it by killing the Gibeonites.

To be fair, God *did* command Saul to destroy his enemies. In obedience, Saul attacked the Philistines, the Moabites, the Ammonites, the Edomites, the Amalekites, and the kings of Zobah, thus delivering Israel from all who had plundered them (1 Samuel 14:47–48). However, Saul overstepped the bounds of God's instructions when he went after the Gibeonites. Now Israel had to endure a three-year famine. The question was: How might this covenant be reinstated?

To make amends, the surviving Gibeonites wanted to hang seven sons of Saul to compensate for what they had suffered under Saul's hand. Not exactly a picnic, but when this was done and their bones had been buried Scripture says, "God answered prayer on behalf of the land" (2 Samuel 21:15). Once both Israel and the Gibeonites were satisfied that the losses had been atoned for, God's blessing returned, and the land began to produce crops once again.

Achan's Sin

Here is another biblical example of what can happen when people break covenants. It also happened shortly after the fall of Jericho.

Prior to the conquest of Jerusalem, the Lord told Israel to devote everything in the city to him. They were to destroy everything and keep no plunder for themselves. Everyone followed these instructions to the letter, except for a man named Achan. He decided to keep a nice robe for himself as well as some gold and silver.

The next city the Israelites attacked was Ai. It was a small settlement compared to Jericho, so Joshua sent only 3,000 men to deal with it. But the Lord did not go with the soldiers into this battle, and they were defeated. When Joshua inquired about the defeat, the Lord replied,

> *Stand up! What are you doing down on your face? Israel has sinned; they have violated my covenant, which I commanded them to keep. They have taken some of the devoted things; they have stolen, they have lied, they have put them with their own possessions. That is why the Israelites cannot stand against their enemies; they turn their backs and run because they have been made liable to destruction. I will not be with you any more unless you destroy whatever among you is devoted to destruction. (Joshua 7:10–13)*

Just as in Saul's case, Achan's act of disobedience broke the deal with God and opened a gap in the wall for the enemy to come in! And, like Saul, his inability to pass up a few trinkets did not just affect him but all the people of Israel.

As you can see, breaking an agreement brings about serious consequences. Just like Israel, God's covenant of protection had been removed from Switzerland when the government and the banks backed out of the deal. As I continued to follow this story, a number of other things occurred, revealing more of the Lord's fingerprints in the midst of the tragedy.

Can you organize these events into a prophetic timeline?

On December 7, 1999 the Virkler Commission completed its work. They found 54,000 accounts that could be linked to holocaust victims—a far cry from the 775 accounts the Swiss banks had owned up to a few years earlier. In addition, another two million dormant accounts were discovered from that era but without the necessary documentation to prove Jewish ownership. This report tarnished the Swiss banks' reputations. Now they had to change some of the laws guarding their much coveted financial independence and secrecy. Once again, the Lord was humbling the proud.

As we have discussed previously, it is important to watch the timing of events and their proximity to each other. In this case, the dates go like this:

- August 23, 1998 - Swiss government and Swiss National Bank back out of deal
- August 28, 1998 – Breakdown in Swiss/Israeli relations
- September 1, 1998 – Sanctions against Swiss were set to go in effect
- September 3, 1998 – Swissair crash
- September 5 1998 – Swiss Ambassador to Canada hit by train
- December 7, 1999 – Virkler Report complete
- December 9, 1999 – Final ceremony for Swissair passengers

Isn't it remarkable how the dates parallel each other? On December 7, the Virkler Commission filed its report on some four million accounts in 59 banks. The biggest bank audit of all time was complete. Two days later, the final ceremony was held at Peggy's Cove, bringing closure to the lives that were lost in the Swissair crash. What are the odds of that? Astronomical, in my opinion, unless someone behind the scenes was calling the shots, calling his people to watch and pray.

*Is there evidence of a paradigm-shift, particularly from pride to humility,
in the people involved?*

With the judgment of God now falling on the nation of Switzerland,
I began to watch for abnormal activity, things that would seem to be
out of the national character. If God had spoken, events should still
unfold in such a way that there was a clear call for a change in national
identity, a paradigm-shift from pride to humility. One sign of a people
under judgment is being given over to hardness of heart and sin. As
the Bible says,

> *"For although they knew God, they neither glorified him as God
> nor gave thanks to him, but their thinking became futile and their
> foolish hearts darkened.... Therefore God gave them over to the
> sinful desires of their hearts." (Romans 1:21,24)*

Seeing as I had just scratched the surface on the nation of Switzerland,
it was difficult to see all the ramifications the Swiss government's refusal
to humble itself would have. To refuse to humble yourself is to harden
your heart. What would be some obvious results of this hardening? When
God speaks, things change. This change can be seen in the attitudes and
hearts of the people with whom God is dealing. We saw this when we
looked at England. Things changed with the English on every level. The
same sort of change could be seen in Switzerland as well, except that
Switzerland refused a new paradigm and chose instead to harden their
hearts and find excuses as to why their paradigm should stay the same.
One result I could see immediately was an increased hatred of foreigners. This was evident in the following general election, when support
for the far-right, anti-immigrant, Holocaust-denying SVP party grew
substantially. A survey done around the 1998 election found that anti-
Semitism also remained deeply rooted in the country, with 16 percent
of Swiss people admitting they were fundamentally anti-Semitic and 60
percent saying they had some anti-Semitic sympathies.[22]

It seemed like instead of humbling themselves, Switzerland decided
to blame others for their mistakes, thus hardening their hearts. Hatred
of foreigners grew, partly because the nation refused to admit it was

wrong and take collective responsibility for what it had done to the Jews. By 2004, the right-wing Swiss People's Party, a political party that ran on a platform that foreigners were criminals and drug addicts won 27 percent of the popular vote making it the largest single political party in the Swiss parliament.[23] Things didn't have to go that way. The Swiss had a choice. If they had just admitted their guilt and dealt with it, they could have had peace. Instead, the Swiss chose the other way, leading only to more bitterness and accusations. If this pattern isn't halted, racial friction and the problems it causes will only escalate. This wound that should have been cleaned and healed has been left to fester and grow.

As time progressed, more pieces were added to the puzzle. The Swiss government created a committee to prove the Jews wrong. They were confident this international committee would study Switzerland's activities during the war and prove they had done nothing wrong. Unfortunately for the Swiss, the results of the committee merely reaffirmed what God had been saying all along, as this news article recounts.

Swiss blame greed for WW2 sins

TORONTO, March 23, 2002: A lengthy study of Switzerland's policies during the Second World War has shattered the picture of a tiny haven seeking peace through neutrality, portraying instead a country that saw the war as a prime opportunity to make a quick profit.

The study was commissioned by the Swiss government in hopes of countering damaging claims by Jewish groups. But it backfired, finding instead that Switzerland committed "quite egregious failures" during the war, including sending thousands of refugees to their deaths in Nazi Germany and using its neutrality to reap huge profits from Germany and Italy.

The authors of the exhaustive five-year study note the Swiss were not motivated by pro-Nazi sympathies, but mainly by greed.

Released yesterday in Bern, the report strongly condemned the country's wartime refugee policy. It accused Switzerland of "excessive" co-operation with the Nazis and criticized its failure to return assets to their rightful owners after the war.

Researched and written by nine historians, lawyers and economists, the report explodes long-held myths about the country that is the birthplace of the Red Cross and is liked around the world for its chocolate and its cuckoo clocks.

Its work supports allegations, made mostly by Jewish groups during the past decade, that Switzerland and its banks took advantage of the country's neutrality and banking secrecy laws to reap enormous profits amid wartime destruction and human misery.

The bitter debate between Swiss officials and Jewish groups over unclaimed Jewish assets held in Swiss bank vaults resulted in the country's biggest banks paying US$1.25 billion in 1998 to settle all Holocaust-era claims.[24]

The false paradigm that God had been after was finally displayed for the world to see. But that has not prevented the Swiss from delaying payment and access to information for as long as they can. This story is still unfolding today. In January 2005, Swiss banks released a new list of 3,100 names of account owners who may have been Nazi victims. However, even though many Holocaust survivors see this as a symbolic victory, one huge part of the puzzle is still missing: an apology. "The Swiss banks have taken too long to publish the lists," Leo Rechter, 77, secretary of Holocaust Survivors Foundation USA said. "The average Holocaust survivor thinks they are waiting for all of us to die so they can do whatever they want with the money." Said another Holocaust survivor, "What is important with these settlements is not the money. We... are trying to achieve a symbolic acknowledgment, a measure of justice."[25]

How does God want me to respond?

While it appears justice is finally being served on one level, the Swiss still seem like they are a long way off from humbling themselves. Here is the gap in which we need to stand in on behalf of the Swiss. Rather than gloat and await their doom, as prophetic intercessors we must pray instead for humility and healing. We need to stand in the gaps surrounding Switzerland that the nation's poor decisions have opened. We need to cry out for the mercy of God. We need to involve ourselves with the Great Author as he writes his history in this country. As God's timeline of events progresses, we need to keep pace by watching. We will know what to pray for as we put the pieces of his puzzle together.

Watching and Praying

After reading through these three case studies, I hope you are convinced that *watching* is a vital part of praying. God wants us to seek out the holes in the walls of nations, churches, and individual lives. Just as David and Joshua found out why God's blessing had dried up, it is our job as prophetic intercessors today to find these gaps and fill them with prayer. The Church needs to work with God on the earth as he works with Man and the leaders of men. God wants his Bride to be involved in watching and praying.

Let us continue to read the writings of the Great Author, gaining hope and faith in his redemptive work. He is in control, and we are to partner with him through prayer as his hand moves throughout the nations. Above all, let us believe that God can work all things together for good. Even in the midst of horrible events, he can give us signs of his plan of redemption and involve us with that plan through prayer for the good of humankind.

---

[1] "No Survivors in Canada air Crash," http://news.bbc.co.uk/1/hi/world/americas/163662.stm (September 3, 1998).

[2] "Swiss ambassador crushed by train," *The Ottawa Citizen*, September 6, 1998, p. B1.

[3] John Gill (Onlinebible.org) February 22, 2005.

[4] Leon Morris, *The Gospel According to Luke* (Grand Rapids: Eerdmans, 2002) p. 326.

[5] The Swiss are world famous for their banking, especially if you need to get money out of your own country and into a safe, anonymous place.

[6] "Hearing on the Swiss Banks and the 1946 Washington Accords*" Senate Banking, Housing and Urban Affairs Committee* http://banking.senate.gov/98_07hrg/072298/witness/ziegler.htm (July 22, 1998).

[7] Jean Ziegler, *The Swiss, the Gold, and the Dead* (New York: Harcourt Brace, 1997) p. 69.

[8] "54,000 Swiss Accounts Tied to the Nazis War Victims," *The New York Times* December 7, 1999, p. A17.

[9] Gregg Rickman, *Swiss Banks and Jewish Souls* (Transaction Pub, 1999) p. 231.

[10] "Guard Who Turned over Swiss Banking Files Seeks Protection in U.S. Senate," http://edition.cnn.com/US/9705/07/swiss.guard/index.html, (January 5, 2005).

[11] Gregg Rickman, *Swiss Banks and Jewish Souls* (Transaction Publications, 1999) p. 217.

[12] "Israeli Survivors Seek to Keep Options Open Against Swiss National Bank," *Jerusalem Post,* September 20, 1998, p. 4.

[13] Gregg Rickman, *Swiss Banks and Jewish Souls* (Transaction Pub, 1999), p. 222.

[14] Ibid, p. 223.

[15] "Netanyahu's Letter to Bronfman Irritates Swiss," *Nue Zurich Zeteitung* (Swiss Week in Review), September 21–27, 1998.

[16] "Netanyahu Abruptly Cancels Working Visit to Switzerland," *Nue Zurich Zeteitung* (Swiss Week In Review), November 23–28, 1998.

[17] Tom Bower, *Nazi Gold* (New York: HarperCollins, 1997) p. 328.

[18] Gregg Rickman, *Swiss Banks and Jewish Souls* (Transaction Pub, 1999), p. 231.

[19] "Swiss President Says Pleas for a Holocaust fund are 'Blackmail'," *New York Times,* January 1, 1997.

[20] "Swiss National Bank Spurns Holocaust Fund," *New York Times*, August 22, 1998.

[21] Gregg Rickman, *Swiss Banks and Jewish Souls* (Transaction Pub, 1999) p. 227.

[22] "Swiss Anti-Semitism Deeply Rooted," http://news.bbc.co.uk/1/hi/world/europe/678669.stm. (March 15, 2000).

[23] "Swiss Right in Political Avalanche," http:news.bbc.co.uk/2/hi/Europe/3204412.stm (October 20, 2003).

[24] "Swiss Blame Greed for WWII Sins," *National Post,* March 23, 2002, p. A1.

[25] http://www.libertypost.org/cgi-bin/readart.cgi?ArtNum=81280.

Conclusion

FAITH vs. FEAR

God is in charge of the earth, he always has been, and he always will be. The problem has never been that we have a small, powerless God. As I have tried to demonstrate in this book, the problem is that we have been made to feel small and powerless by our inability to see our great and mighty God at work. We have forgotten our native language, the symbolic language of God. We have forgotten how God communicated with his prophets. We have forgotten how to *watch* as Jesus commanded us to do. Thankfully, some language lessons like the ones you have just read in this book easily rectify this problem. All we need to do is re-learn the symbolic language of God, the language of dream and vision, sign and wonder.

The question for us now is not whether God speaks or whether he has the power to intervene in the affairs of the world, but how badly we want to know what God is up to? How eager are we to see him display his power? Do we want to learn the language of God merely so we can "pass the test," as many of us did with French or Spanish in high school? Or, like someone who has married a spouse from another country and culture, do we want to learn the language of God so we can relate to the Lover of our souls on the most intimate level imaginable?

God wants us to learn his language so we can follow him as he continues to write the story of humankind. God wants us to know his language so we can see that he, our Beloved, is with us and for us and has never left us or forsaken us.

A Final Story

To help emphasize how important this, I would like to close with a remarkable experience God used to teach me this very lesson. But first, a few words by way of introduction: When bad things continue to happen, we tend to jump to one of two conclusions, both of which are often incorrect:

1) The devil is out to get me.
2) God is out to get me (I am being judged for sin).

Lurking at the heart of both of these conclusions is the same, nasty little four-letter word: *fear*. Hence, there is a third option I would like you to consider:

3) God, as a loving Father, is working to transform you into the image of his Son.

Now the Lord is the Spirit, and where the Spirit of the Lord is, there is freedom. And we, who with unveiled faces all reflect the Lords' glory, are being transformed into his likeness with ever increasing glory, which comes for the Lord, who is the Spirit. (2 Corinthians 3:17–18)

I know that God loves me; that he is Abba Father, "Daddy," meaning I have nothing to fear from him or the enemy. So what is my response when bad things happen over and over again? How do I live in such a way so that even though the world around me is broken and full of fear, I can still find the God of love? Here is a personal example that I believe will hit the mark.

Dealing With Crows

One day while driving in the country, I saw an eagle sitting on the very tip of a hemlock tree. It was a strange place for an eagle to rest, I thought, because the tip of the tree was so thin, it was nearly doubled over under his weight. Then, as I watched, a crow swooped in and tried to dislodge the eagle from his perch. The crow dived, flipped, flapped, and cawed. But no matter how angry the crow got, the eagle remained calm. Something told me to pay attention to this strange event. I wondered: Did this mean I was about to be harassed just like that eagle?

The next morning, I spent some time reading at home. It was shaping up to be a beautiful day; the sun was just burning its way through the clouds. As I looked out the window, I noticed a squirrel sitting on top of a telephone pole. This was not an unusual sight. Squirrels roam constantly across our property. However, this squirrel wasn't moving. In fact, I thought it might be dead. I glanced up at it every once in a while to see if it had moved, but it remained exactly where it was, stock still, it's little face pointing in my direction. Finally, I decided to go out and take a look at this strange squirrel. Being the energetic creatures they are, my only conclusion was that it must have died while waiting for the sun to come out.

I put on my coat and stepped outside. At that moment, it was as if a film director yelled, "Action!" The squirrel began to run as fast as he could down the telephone wire with a crow in fast pursuit. Swooping in from the left and the right, the crow tried to knock the squirrel off the wire! The squirrel was quick, but not quick enough. The crow gave him a glancing blow, and he slipped off the wire, only managing to grab on at the last minute and pull himself back up. The squirrel must have decided that the wire was a bad idea, so he made a mammoth leap into a tree fifteen feet away. Once he was safe in its branches, he turned and chattered a blue streak at the crow.

As I watched this, all I could think was, two days in a row I had seen a crow harass another animal. What were the odds of that? Was this just a coincidence or was God trying to tell me something? I didn't like the idea of being harassed! This couldn't be God, because it made me feel nervous and fearful. No, this was definitely not God. It only produced bad fruit—lack of peace. "Get away from me, Satan!" I thought. "This is my day off!"

The next day, it was time to go back to class. I had conveniently forgotten about the crows, but it appeared the Great Writer had not forgotten about me. It was time for act three.

As my friend Diane and I were driving toward church, we saw a strange sight in the sky: Two crows were at war. They were locked beak-to-beak, foot-to-foot, tumbling toward the ground. They were probably 100 yards up and another 100 yards down the road from us. I glanced at the road for a second then back at the crows. They were still falling, still locked in their battle of wills.

And then the bizarre happened. When the crows reached tree level, I realized they were falling directly toward my van. It was too late to swerve out of the way. All I could do was watch as their epic battle came to a colossal end—taking my windshield with it! That's right, the crows fell out of the sky and scored a bull's eye on my windshield—killing themselves in the process!

I was freaked. Three days in a row, three incidents with crows! What were the odds of that? What bad thing was coming my way? Now my paradigm was controlled completely by fear! I was certain I was about to come under some huge demonic assault. I was about to get harassed, and maybe worse! Why? What had I done to deserve this?

Off to Class

As you can imagine, this event was the first thing we discussed when we arrived at class. What a great example of what we were learning. I don't think I had ever arrived with material that was so fresh.

Thankfully, after hearing my story, my friend Brad Jersak gave me a smack in the head that helped me think a little clearer. "God doesn't show us things to cause fear; we both agree on that, don't we?" He said.

"Right," I agreed, in a nervous voice.

"So let's take this apart," Brad continued. "What do you associate with crows?"

"Curses," I said.

"Okay," Brad responded. "Now, as you've taught us, vehicles often represent the direction in which we are traveling. So the way I look at this, you are about to kill some nasty curses on your life, just like you killed those crows."

"Hmm… That interpretation is much better than mine," I murmured, my face brightening a little.

"What do you associate with windows?" Brad asked, a big smile on his face. He was smiling because he already knew the answer. I had taught the class that paradigms are like eyeglasses or windows through which we view the world. Now Brad had me just where he wanted me. "I would suggest that God is about to break a false belief system in your life that is affecting your ministry. In a place you feel you are under a curse, that curse is about to break."

Wow. I couldn't believe how hopeful his interpretation of these events was. What a contrast to my fear-based interpretation, which simply left me feeling powerless.

I was feeling a little better, but I still wondered how the timeline of events would unfold. As it turns out, I didn't need to wait for long.

Here is a little bit of background so you will understand the next two weeks of my life: When I burned out and left the church years earlier (as recounted in chapter three), many of my relationships had suffered as a result. Some people blamed me for God Rock's demise. Others were simply angry with me for leaving. My relationship with the former senior pastor was also in a state of disrepair. Before I resigned, I told him I felt God was leading me to start a prophetic school. He didn't think it was a good idea; in fact he and his wife were urging Kelly and I to pastor a church in Ontario. Kelly and I didn't think that was right for us though, and this caused a break in our relationship. It also affected how I related to his five daughters, three of whom had been home group leaders at God Rock.

Since leaving God Rock, I had tried to avoid these people. But after the crow incidents, suddenly they were everywhere. I went for a jog in the park and ran into one of the pastor's daughters and her husband, both of whom used to be home group leaders. I ran right on by with a smile on my face. At church a few days later, the pastor's eldest daughter sat down in my row two chairs over. As I walked into the coffee shop

I liked to frequent, I saw one of the pastor's younger daughters, who had begun working behind the counter.

On it went, with former home group leaders popping up everywhere, often a few times per day. I knew God was pushing my buttons through this, but why? At this point, I had not made a connection between these meetings and the crows smashing through my windshield. I knew I was feeling shame and guilt when I saw those people, but I thought those feelings were well deserved under the circumstances. I had not measured up to people's expectations. Why shouldn't they be upset with me?

One night, I thought going to the movies would be a great diversion. That is, until I ran into the senior pastor's other two daughters in the theatre. It was as if I was being followed! Then, while standing in the food line, I turned around and saw the senior pastor standing right behind me! It was an awkward moment, but we both managed to smile and make small talk. However, as I walked back to my seat, I couldn't help thinking, *what were the odds of that?*

Two days later, one of the senior pastor's daughters dropped off a wedding invitation at my house. I couldn't believe it. Now I would have to face all of these people whether I liked it or not. I was beginning to think there was a divine conspiracy afoot to compound my guilt. However, even though everything was telling me to run away, I knew I had to kill this thing. I needed a new paradigm, a new way of seeing the world.

An Unexpected Reception

Kelly and I were tense as we drove to the reception. Who was going to be there? How would they react when they saw us? What were we going to say?

When I walked in, my eyes lit upon five of my old home group leaders huddled together at a table. They waited until Kelly and I found a table and then began moving toward us. The moment of truth had arrived.

I had expected judgment. What I received instead was friendship. Instead of condemning me, they embraced me and told me how much they missed me, and that they were glad to see me. We even talked of the good times. I had honestly forgotten a good deal of them (burnout does weird things to your mind). However, my mind caught this much: These people didn't judge me, they loved me. It was a pleasant surprise to say the least.

As the night went on, I continued to reconcile with a number of people from God Rock. When things had quieted down and the happy couple was off, even the senior pastor came over to talk. He told me that he had heard about the prophetic school and that it was going well. Then he told me I was right to start it, that he was wrong, and that he was proud of me. I couldn't believe it! After everything that had happened, he was proud of me!

After that event, I began to feel love and trust coming back, the ability to dream and believe things would work out. And then it hit me: I understood what the incident with the crow and the eagle was about, I understood about the squirrel, I understood about the two crows smashing through my windshield. I was like the eagle being harassed by feelings of failure, of starting a ministry that was not blessed by my spiritual father. These false beliefs were the crows, constantly nagging at me and stealing my peace. But now I had defeated these lies, the crows were dead. I had a new belief system, just like I now had a new windshield in my van. I could see the path clearly in front of me knowing I was forgiven, embraced, and in the center of God's will.

Crow Post-mortem

This experience illustrates a rule of thumb that always holds true: When things continue to go wrong, don't take it as a sign that doom is just around the corner. Instead, realize that such signs are God's way of speaking to us about things in our lives that need to change so we can become like Jesus. Think about Jonah. When God killed the vine and supplied the wind and the scorching sun, God wasn't trying to scare Jonah. He was trying to help Jonah see the condition of his heart. The same holds true for us today. God is constantly removing the old to make way for the new. Transition and transformation have come. When bad things happen, look at the circumstances of your life. Is anything pushing your buttons? If so, that means you have a button to push! God wants to disconnect it and remove it! God wants to install new things in your life, and when it is time, signs of this new growth will abound as well!

It is time to pick up the inheritance God promised his people in Acts 2, the language of the prophets. It is time to begin reading the Great Author's modern works. God wants us to know that he is in control of the affairs of humankind, and he wants all of us to play a part in his epic tale.

> *Praise be to the name of God forever and ever; wisdom and power are his. He changes times and seasons; he sets up kings and deposes them. He gives wisdom to the wise and knowledge to the discerning. (Daniel 2:20–21)*

It is also time we begin seeing the language of God through the eyes of Jesus. We need to believe that God speaks through signs but refrains from interpreting these events through the eyes of the enemy or the eyes of Man. Man's eyes scoff at the writings of the Great Author, and the devil's eyes distort everything written by the finger of God into a paradigm of fear. But…

> *You did not receive a Spirit that makes you a slave again to fear, but you received the Spirit of sonship. And we cry out Abba, Father. (Romans 8:15)*

> *There is no fear in love. But perfect love drives out all fear, because fear has to do with punishment. The man who fears is not made perfect in love. (1 John 4:18)*

Thus, it is only when we see the world from the point of view of the Bride and Groom that the language of God begins to look and sound like the language of heaven. This is the paradigm we must develop: to see the Groom everywhere we look.

Bibliography

Articles

"54,000 Swiss Accounts Tied to the Nazis War Victims," *The New York Times,* December 7, 1999.

"Al Eyes International Panel on Nazi Gold," *Daily News,* June 2, 1998.

"A Gamble With History," *Time Magazine,* October 27, 1997.

"AIADMK Ministers Resign," http://www.tribuneindia.com/1999/99apro7/ (April 7, 1999).

"All About Britain," http://www.bbcamerica.com/britain/queen_1990.jsp (1999).

"Amid Debt, Doubt and Secrecy, Hussein and Rabin Made Peace," *The New York Times,* July 31, 1994, p 1.

"Atal Invited to Form Govt.," http://www.tribuneindia.com/1999/99oct12/head.htm#1 (October 12, 1999).

"Audit Aims to Find Dormant Accounts of Nazi Victims," http://edition.cnn.com/WORLD/9611/19/swiss.gold/index.html (November 19, 1996).

"Bank of Japan Buying into America," *USA Today*, April 21, 1995.

"Britain's Queen to Hire 'Spin Doctor',"
    http://archives.cnn.com/1998WORLD/europe/02/22/
    queen/index.html (February 22, 1998).

"Britannia Sets sail for Farewell Voyage,"
    http://edition.cnn.com/WORLD/9710/20/brittania/
    index.html (October 20, 1997).

"Briton's Royals Hold Management Meeting,"
    http://edition.cnn.com/WORLD/9609/17/britain.royal/
    index.html (September 17, 1996).

"Cats and Cat-calls During President's Speech,"
    http://www.indiaexpress.com/archive_frame.php
    (February 23, 1999).

"Compassion and 'Hard Choices' An Interview With Britain's Prime
    Minister," *Time Magazine*, October 27, 1997.

"D'Amato: Documents Show Swiss Shipped 188 Tons of Nazi Gold
    to Portugal, Spain," http://banking.senate.gov/issues/swiss/
    prel97/021997.htm (February 19, 1997).

"Downsizing the House of Windsor," *The New York Times*, August 25,
    1996, p. 4.

"Fire Damages Windsor Castle," *The Vancouver Sun*, Nov 21, 1992, p.
    A15.

"Fired Swiss Guard Responds to Bank's Admission,"
    http://edition.cnn.com/US/9811/20/swiss.guard/
    (November 20, 1998).

"Government Will Survive, say PM,"
http://www.tibuneindia.com/1999/99apri07/head.htm#3
(April 7, 1999).

"Guard Who Turned over Swiss Banking Files Seeks Protection
in U.S. Senate," http://edition.cnn.com/US/9705/07/
swiss.guard/index.html (May 7, 1997).

"Hearing on the Swiss Banks and the 1946 Washington Accords,"
Senate Banking, Housing and Urban Affairs Committee
http://banking.senate.gov/98_07hrg/072298/witness/
ziegler.htm (July 22, 1998).

"India's Prime Minister Expected to Resign After Government Loses
Confidence Vote," http://edition.cnn.com/world/asiapcf/
9904/india.01/index.html.

"Israeli Survivors Seek to Keep Options Open Against Swiss
National Bank," *Jerusalem Post,* September 20, 1998, p. 4.

"Israel Returns Jordan Royal Steed," *The Province,*
April 10, 1992, p. A31.

"Japan-Relations With the United States,"
http://countrystudies.us/japan/ (1992).

"Memorandum of Understanding between the World Jewish Restitution Organization and the World Jewish Congress representing also the Jewish Agency and Allied Organizations and the
Swiss Bankers Association," http://www.switzerland.taskforc
e.ch/ (May 2, 1996).

"Netanyahu Abruptly Cancels Working Visit to Switzerland," *Nue Zurich Zeteitung* (Swiss Week In Review), Nov 23–28 1998.

"Netanyahu's Letter to Bronfman Irritates Swiss," *Nue Zurich Zeteitung* (Swiss Week in Review), Sept 21–27 1998.

"New Look Windsor for New Look Monarchy," http://news.bbc.co.uk/1/hi/32057.stm (November 17, 1997).

"New Pressure On Swiss to Solve Mystery of Nazi Gold," http://edition.cnn.com/WORLD/9609/18/swiss.gold/index.html. (September 18, 1996).

"No Survivors in Canada air Crash," http://news.bbc.co.uk/1/hi/world/americas/163662.stm (September 3, 1998).

"On Her Majesty's Service," *Daily Telegraph,* January 31, 1998.

"Polo Pony High-tails it to Israel," *Daily News,* April 8, 1992, p. 17.

"President's Rule in Bihar Revoked," http://www.tibuneindia.com/1999/99mar09/ (March 9, 1999).

"Princess Diana: The Earl's daughter, born to life of privilege," http://www.cnn.com/WORLD/9708/diana/earls.daughter/index.html (1997).

"Public Deserting Prince of Wales,"
    http://www.telegraph.co.uk/portal/main.html.

"Queen Promises to Modernize Monarchy,"
    http://news.bbc.co.uk/1/hi/uk/33290.stm
    (November 20, 1997).

"Revealed: How Swiss Banks Swindled the Heirs of Holocaust Victims," *Daily Telegraph,* December 5, 1999.

"Royal Jordanian Horse Swims from Akaba to Eilat," *Jerusalem Post,* April 8, 1992, p. A1.

"Separate Lives." *Time Magazine,* November 30, 1992.

"Stunned Japanese Offer Sympathy as Some are Struck by Symbolism," *The New York Times,* January 9, 1992, p. A8.

"Swatch Boss Calls for Boycott of U.S. over Nazi-gold Flap," *New York Post,* July 12, 1998.

"Swiss ambassador crushed by train," *The Ottawa Citizen,* September 6, 1998, p. B1.

"Swiss Anti-Semitism Deeply Rooted,"
    http://news.bbc.co.uk/1/hi/world/europe/678669.stm.
    (March 15, 2000).

"Swiss Bank Shreds War-Era Data But a Suspicious Guard Halts It," *New York Times,* January 15, 1997.

"Swiss Blame Greed for WWII Sins," *National Post,* March 23, 2002, p. A1.

"Swiss National Bank Spurns Holocaust Fund," *New York Times*, August 22, 1998.

"Swiss National Bank Won't Participate in Big-Bank Settlement," *Nue Zurich Zeteitung.* (Swiss Week in Review), August 15–21, 1998.

"Swiss President Appeals to Clinton to Stop Sanctions," http://edition.cnn.com/WORLD/europe/9807/23/ swiss.banks/ (July 23, 1998).

"Swiss to Move Quickly on Compensating Jews for Stolen Gold," http://edition.cnn.com/WORLD/9701/12/briefs.pm/ swiss.html (January 12, 1997).

"Swiss to Pay Jews 1.25 billion, Holocaust Victims. Kin to Benefit," *Daily News,* August 13, 1998.

"Swiss President Says Pleas for a Holocaust fund are 'Blackmail'," *New York Times*, January 1, 1997.

"Swiss Right in Political Avalanche," http:news.bbc.co.uk/2/hi/ Europe/3204412.stm (October 20, 2003).

"Swiss Vote to Retain Gold," http://news.bbc.co.uk/1/hi/world/europe/2274653.stm (September 22, 2002).

"Switzerland and the Holocaust Assets," http://www.giussani.com/holocaust-assets/welcome.html.

"The Changing Face of the Monarchy," http://news.bbc.co.uk/1/hi/special_report/1998/diana/ 59991.stm (April 25, 1998).

"The Queen Bows to Her People," *Daily Telegraph,*
    September 5, 1997.

"The Queen's Year of Joy and Woe," *Daily Telegraph,*
    December 26, 1997.

"U.S. Financial Community Set to Sanction Swiss on Nazi Gold,"
    http://edition.cnn.com/US/9807/02/swiss.holocaust.gold/
    index.html (July 2, 1998).

"Windsor Castle Reopens Five Years After Devastating Fire"
    http://edition.cnn.com/WORLD/9712/27/windsor.castle/
    index.html (December 27, 1997).

"With Brightest Star Gone Royals Face an Uncertain Future,"
    http://edition.cnn.com/WORLD/9708/31/diana.star.dies/
    (August 31, 1997).

Books

Beers, Gilbert, *The Book of Life.* Grand Rapids: Zondervan, 1980.

Bower, Tom, *Nazi Gold.* New York: Harper Collins, 1997.

Clayton, Tim and Craig, Phil, *Diana: The Story of a Princess.* New York:
    Pocket Books, 2001.

Davis, John, *Moses and the Gods of Egypt.* Grand Rapids: Baker Books,
    1971.

Enns, Peter, *Exodus: The New Application Commentary.* Grand Rapids:
    Zondervan, 2000.

Fretheim, Terence, *Exodus: A Bible Commentary for Teaching and Preaching*. Louisville: John Knox Press, 1991.

Gahlin, Lucia, *The Myths and Mythology of Ancient Egypt*. London: Annes Publications, 2003.

Gill, John, *Expository Bible Commentary*, http://www.onlinebible.org/html/eng/index.htm.

Henry, Matthew, *Mathew Henry's Commentary on the Whole Bible*. Peabody Mass: Hendrickson's Publishers, 1991.

Itamar, Levin, *The Last Deposit, Swiss Banks and Holocaust Accounts*. Westpost Ct.: Praeger Publications, 1999.

Lacy, Robert. Royal: *Her Majesty Queen Elizabeth II*. London: Little, Brown 2002.

Maxie, Dunham D., *Exodus: The Communicator's Commentary*. USA: W Publishing Group, 1987.

Morris, Leon, *The Gospel According to Luke*. Grand Rapids: Eerdmans, 2002.

Morton, Andrew, *Diana, Her New Life*. New York: Simon and Schuster, 1994.

Nicolson, Adam, *Restoration: The Rebuilding of Windsor Castle*. London: M. Joseph, 1997.

Rickman, Gregg, *Swiss Banks and Jewish Souls*. New Brunswick: Transaction Publishing, 1999.

Sarna, Nahum, *Exploring Exodus—The Heritage of Biblical Israel*. New York: Schoken Books, 1986.

Schlossstein, Steven, *The End of the American Century*. New York: Congdon & Weed, 1989.

Smith, William, *OT History: From Creation to the Return*. New York: College Press, 1990.

Wilkins, Michael, *Exodus: NIV Application Commentary*. Grand Rapids: Zondervan, 2004.

Ions, Veronica, *Library of the Worlds' Myths and Religions*. New York: Deter Berick Books, 1982.

Goll, Jim, *Study Notes: Handling Dreams, Visions, and Revelations*. Ministry to the Nations, p. 28.

Ziegler, Jean, *The Swiss, the Gold, and the Dead*. New York: Harcourt Brace & Co., 1998.

Acknowledgements

This book could not have happened without the people who believe in me and walk with me.

The Langley Vineyard: Thanks for letting me begin again.

My Samuel's Mantle students: Thank you for pushing me to get this done and funding it so it would become done!

Kevin Miller, my editor: Thank you for your brilliance and experience. I cannot express the relief I felt to find an experienced writer who understood what I wanted to put on paper.

Brad Jersak: The most radical guy I know. Thanks for believing in this project and in me even when I didn't.

John and Diane Van Vloten: We have walked together a long ways. You were there when this journey began! Here's to many more journeys.

My wife Kelly, my sons Jesse and Simeon, and my daughter Delci Joy: For us, this is not just theology, it is part of the many ways we listen to God together. What a strange and wonderful journey with the Lord we have had. I couldn't have made it without you. You could always see the treasure when all I saw was dust.

And finally, to Jesus: Thank you for lifting a burned-out pastor from the garbage heap of life, seeing the gold in me, standing me up, and opening my eyes to a whole new way of living. YES, you have sent the Holy Spirit to counsel us, guide us, and lead us into truth! (John 4 &16). Your faithfulness astounds me.

About the Author

A dramatic encounter with God at Youth With a Mission in 1984 was the beginning of a quest for Murray to hear and see God move in his life and the lives of others. This journey led Murray to get his Bachelor of Religious Education from Columbia Bible College (Abbotsford, BC). Following that, he served as an associate pastor at Valley Christian Fellowship in Abbotsford for seven years. During that time, he planted a youth church called God Rock, developed its home group structure, and did itinerant ministry in Canada and the United States. Murray also oversaw the prophetic ministry at Valley Christian Fellowship, mentoring and discipling prophetic people.

Murray and his wife Kelly currently co-lead Samuel's Mantle, a prophetic training school located at Langley Vineyard in Langley, BC. Murray also has an active writing and itinerant speaking ministry. To contact Murray or to book him for a speaking engagement, write to kelmur@shaw.ca.

About Samuel's Mantle

Samuel's Mantle is a prophetic school based at Langley Vineyard in Langley, BC. It is dedicated to seeing the truth of Joel 2 lived out by Christians everywhere.

> *I will pour out my Spirit on all people. Your sons and daughters will prophesy, your old men will dream dreams, you young men will see visions. Even on my servants, both men and women, I will pour out my Spirit in those days. I will show wonders in the heavens and on earth. (Joel 2:28-29)*

Led by Murray and Kelly Dueck and John and Diane Van Vloten, Samuel's Mantle offers three levels of prophetic training classes aimed at equipping the Body of Christ to hear God speak and understand the many ways our Father communicates with us. Classes are structured on a tri-mester system, starting each September.

Several Samuel's Mantle classes are also available on DVD, CD, and audiotape. They can be ordered separately or as a group. For more details on these and other prophetic training resources or to find out how you can get involved with Samuel's Mantle, please visit www.samuelsmantle.com.

www.samuelsmantle.com

Also Available from Fresh Wind Press

CAN YOU HEAR ME?
Tuning In to the God Who Speaks

Can You Hear Me? combines biblical and historical research, real life experiences, and inspiring exercises on "listening prayer" to transform your prayers into intimate conversations—real meetings with a Living Friend.

CHILDREN, CAN YOU HEAR ME?

God loves children and longs to meet with them through prayer. In every daily scenario, he reveals himself freely to kids, speaking to them as a very best Friend.

RIVERS FROM EDEN - 40 Days of Intimate Conversation with God

Rivers from Eden is a forty-day spiritual exercise designed to make "listening prayer" a lifestyle. It models an approach to prayer in which your time with God becomes an intimate, interactive meeting.

FEAR NO EVIL - Breaking Free from the Culture Of Fear

Fear No Evil confronts the culture of fear that surrounds all of us. It begins with snapshots of pop angst then deconstructs the lies that drive fear and offers steps to healing—a spiritual journey into freedom.

www.freshwindpress.com